*The Social History of Poverty:*
*The Urban Experience*

Francesco Cordasco
EDITOR

# THE CITY WILDERNESS

## A SETTLEMENT STUDY

BY

RESIDENTS AND ASSOCIATES OF THE

SOUTH END HOUSE

*Edited by*

ROBERT A. WOODS

*With an Introduction by*

DAVID N. ALLOWAY

GARRETT PRESS, INC.
*New York,* 1970

SBN 512-00794-2
Library of Congress Catalog Card
Number 71-106766

The text of this book is a photographic reprint of the first edition
published in Boston and New York by Houghton, Mifflin and Company in 1898.
Reproduced from a copy in the Garrett Press Collection.

*First Garrett Press Edition Published 1970*

Manufactured in the United States of America

GARRETT PRESS, INC.
*Publishers*

250 West 54th Street, New York, N.Y. 10019

# INTRODUCTION

In the days before the advent of extensive government-operated social services and welfare activity on a large scale, the problems of the poor were the special concern of the private charitable organizations and the consciences of the "better" classes, who often organized special community efforts to do what they could. There were many of these efforts, but perhaps none were more effective than the settlement houses in our major cities which tried to do what they could for the immigrant, the poor, and the friendless.[1]

Historically, settlement houses as an idea were the inspiration of Samuel A. Barnett, vicar of St. Jude's Church in London, in 1884. The concept spread to the United States with the establishment of Toynbee Hall in New York City in 1886. South End Boston, the work of Robert A. Woods and others, followed in 1891.[2] *The City Wilderness* (1898) is a collection of reports and statements available about the Boston house as a broad evaluation of that effort after seven years of operation. Robert A. Woods went on to the executive secretaryship of the National Federation of Settlements in 1911 under the presidency of Jane Addams of Hull House.

Generally, settlement houses brought religious leaders and university students and faculty together in common cause. While they usually concentrated upon a broad band of social welfare problems they were open to people of all

[1]See Jane Addams, *Forty Years at Hull House* (1935) or J.A.R. Pimlott, *Toynbee Hall: Fifty Years of Social Progress, 1884-1935* (1935) for detailed accounts of the whole program and movement.
[2]See Robert A. Woods, *The Neighborhood in Nation-Building* (1923).

races and creeds and were usually neighborhood-oriented in their outlooks, though occasionally a few community centers also began to appear on the scene after 1900.

In many ways the old settlement houses of the late nineteenth century idealists and their predecessors (the genteel reformers) were similar to the Neighborhood Association and Grass Roots Association movements which can be found in many major cities and towns today. Sometimes they are also called Neighborhood Improvement Associations. Basically, the older social constructs sought to get people to act together for the improvement of their neighborhood environments and the conditions of their lives in general. In many ways much emphasis was put upon slum improvement, but the social, and even occasionally the cultural, aspects of their lives were not overlooked. Financed largely by religious groups and staffed by university and college people, they did manage to achieve a great deal of involvement of the people themselves.[3]

The action programs of the settlement houses were geared around the local problems of the neighborhood in which they were to be found, and this gave them a great deal of variety. However, they all seem to have focused on essentially three basic programatic schemata:

(a) Working with individuals and families
(b) Working with the whole neighborhood
(c) Working with neighborhood groups

This was the basic program of settlement houses since their inception in 1884, and they have changed very little since then. They may have become more sophisticated, they

[3]Whenever the term "settlement house" is used, most people respond with the name of Jane Addams as a result of the close relationship she had with Hull House and also as a result of her having been the first president of the National Federation of Settlements (1911). Others who should be mentioned in addition to Robert A. Woods are Lillian D. Wald, Joseph Moss, and Sophonsiba Breckenridge.

may be better financed, and they may be better equipped, but their goals are still pretty much the same, even though they have been having international meetings since 1922, and formed an International Association in 1926.[4]

The activities of the modern neighborhood "settlement" operation are considerably expanded from those of seventy or eighty years ago. Today, in working with individuals the professional services of psychologists and psychiatrists, case workers, vocational counselors, family counselors, and even home economists are employed. Some of the settlement houses now run day-care centers for children of working mothers and others are also in the employment agency business.

The group activities of the houses have probably changed the least. They still seek to develop worthy use of leisure time through recreation facilities for the children and productive group action for the adults which will both improve the neighborhood and the quality of the life of its inhabitants. Self-help groups are still very much encouraged and often supported through the extension of facilities, exepertise, and some limited financial help as well.

Neighborhood action by these activities now leans very heavily on an intervention-type activity in which the "house" acts as the pressure agent for the neighborhood in such vital matters as sanitation, housing code enforcement, and the supportive services of municipal agencies and departments. Some houses also offer legal aid for their neighborhoods and others have even organized neighborhood-store cooperative ventures in group buying to

[4]The first conference was held in London in 1922 and every four years thereafter, except for brief interruption during World War II. After World War II the International Association was headquartered in Paris until 1956, when it moved to Utrecht, Holland, where it has since remained. The Association presently enjoys observer status in the United Nations as a nongovernmental organization.

achieve economic savings through mass purchasing.[5]

Administratively, settlement centers usually are organized under the direction of a board of citizen directors who form the nexus of a private charitable corporation. Some of the directors usually live in the neighborhood itself and the remainder, usually the core of the financial support for the center, is drawn from among the socially minded in the metropolitan area. The make-up of these boards varies considerably, but they usually tend to be fairly sizeable. Charged with making policy, determining budgets and hiring staff, these boards usually solicit the opinions and ideas of the people of the areas they are designed to serve. The staffs of these houses tend to be drawn from the professional ranks of education, social work, and sometimes medicine, and are supplemented by a paraprofessional staff of local neighborhood men and women as far as is possible.

The financial support of these operations varies. Woods and Addams created their settlement houses on church support, and many church groups still support neighborhood activities and operations. Sometimes this is the work of a single congregation, and in the case of the Roman Catholic Church it is often a regular part of a Bishop's budget or the recipient of a large slice of an annual Catholic Charities drive each year. Many others are supported by private gifts (tax deductible incentives are often behind them), or they are part of the regular Community Chest or United Fund drives.[6]

Initially the settlement houses sought to help the newly-arrived immigrant to settle in American life. Because the immigrant had problems with the language, the

[5]See The National Federation of Settlements and Neighborhood Centers, *Neighborhood Centers Today: Action Programs for a Rapidly Changing World* (1960).

[6]See The National Federation of Settlements and Neighborhood Centers, *Standards for Neighborhood Centers* (1960) for more details.

customs, the law, employment, and related matters, he needed a lot of help. This was a prime motivating factor in the settlement house movement. This remained a prime purpose until the restrictive legislation of the 1920's (1921, 1924, and 1929) which drastically cut the flow. However, the depression of the 1930's tended to give these houses a new clientele—the poor in general, and after 1950 the black and Hispanic-American poor.

The settlement house is essentially an urban phenomenon, and they are usually not to be found outside our major cities. It is perhaps ironic to note that in some instances the sons and daughters of the former clients are now the most vigorous opponents of the new clientele of the settlement house—the black American and the Hispanic-American. Almost all of the old settlement houses still remain in operation, as does Woods' South End Boston one, though many have changed their names as they have acquired new functions in the last two or three decades.

Today, as when they first began, the settlement houses continue to seek legislation to help the poor and minority group persons. Sometimes this is new legislation and othertimes it represents simply an amendment to existing legislation to expand the scope, operation, or thrust of it. That the settlement house has played a positive role in the process of nation-building probably cannot effectively be denied, but just what that role is remains still to be effectively assessed.[7] The South End Boston house was an unusually successful one, and Robert Woods was a real pioneer, with Jane Addams, in this whole area of social concern for the poor of the nation.

[7]For two rather penetrating assessments of the settlement house, see Robert A. Woods, *The Neighborhood in Nation Building* (1923) and Robert A. Woods and Albert J. Kennedy, *Settlement Horizon: A National Estimate* (1922).

The serious student of the settlement house can find much useful information about the settlement house phenomenon in general by examining the official reports of such groups as South End House, Toynbee Hall, Hull House and the College Settlement of New York City. Biographies of Jane Addams, Robert Woods, Lillian Wald, and others, as available, would shed additional information and light on the kinds of individuals who sparked these activities.

In addition to the works cited in the footnotes, the reader should consult Mary K. Simkhovitch, *Neighborhood: My Story of Greenwich House* (1938); Graham Taylor, *Pioneering on Social Frontiers* (1930), and his *Chicago Commons, Through Forty Years* (1936), or Lillian Wald's *Windows on Henry Street* (1934). Other dimensions of the matter are explored in Lorene M. Pacey (ed.), *Readings in the Development of Settlement Work* (1950), Fern M. Colborn, *Buildings of Tomorrow: Guide for Planning Settlements and Community Buildings* (1955). From the point of view of social welfare, the settlement house can also be studied in Emerson F. Andrews, *Philanthropic Giving* (1950), Isaac M. Rubinow, *The Quest for Security* (1934), Frederick Watkins, *The Political Tradition of the West* (1948), and H.C. Wilensky & C.N. Lebeaux, *Industrial Society and Social Welfare* (1958), as well as through the great mass of social welfare publications, documents, reports, studies, and monographs available from the U.S. Department of Health, Education and Welfare.

David N. Alloway
*Montclair State College*

# THE
# CITY WILDERNESS

## A SETTLEMENT STUDY

BY

RESIDENTS AND ASSOCIATES OF THE
SOUTH END HOUSE

EDITED BY
## ROBERT A. WOODS
HEAD OF THE HOUSE

### SOUTH END
### BOSTON

BOSTON AND NEW YORK
HOUGHTON, MIFFLIN AND COMPANY
The Riverside Press, Cambridge
1898

# PREFACE

In the autumn of 1891, Professor William J. Tucker, then of the Theological Seminary at Andover, now president of Dartmouth College, sent out a circular in which he proposed that there should be established in one of the more crowded districts of Boston a house " designed to stand for the single idea of resident study and work." The singleness of this idea has ever since been the guiding principle of the settlement which came of that initial effort. The present volume is simply a larger development succeeding a series of bulletins which have presented from year to year the hard-won gains of actual experience.

The writers of this volume have all been citizens of the South End of Boston for considerable periods. With one exception, they have been in residence at the South End House. Each writer has devoted himself specially to those topics with which his local interests have made him the most conversant. To the editor has fallen the duty of directing the investigation, and of approving and unifying its results. In this he has had the constant coöperation of his colleague in the executive work of the settlement, Mr. William I. Cole. Two of the chapters are by a writer who withholds his name, out of consideration for certain interests that involve outside persons.

At every stage in the investigation the writers have had the assistance of public officials, trade-union leaders, philanthropic workers, and other persons familiar with the past and present of the South End. Mr. Horace G. Wadlin, chief, and Mr. Charles F. Pidgin, chief clerk, of the State Bureau of Statistics of Labor, have given special assistance in connection with the statistical groundwork of the investigation. Mr. O. M. Hanscom, Deputy Superintendent of Police for the southern districts, has made accessible much important information in the police records. Professor W. J. Ashley, of Harvard University, kindly read most of the manuscript in an early stage, and gave a number of profitable suggestions. For some of the more subtle human aspects of the local life the writings of Mr. Alvan F. Sanborn, long one of the settlement group, have been to some extent drawn upon, and references are given at the appropriate places for those who may wish to go further in that direction. Two other valued

former residents have made contributions to the
volume in its final form. Professor Henry G.
Pearson, of the English department in the Massachusetts Institute of Technology, has read the
whole of the proof, and many places in the text
show his critical skill. Mr. M. A. de Wolfe Howe
supplied what may be little to give but is much
to receive, the title. The phrase was first used
by Mr. Howe in an article in the "Atlantic
Monthly" for January, 1896. Several of the
younger associates of the house have assisted in
particular ways, — Mr. R. W. Babson, in connection with certain economic inquiries; Mr. F. Q.
Blanchard, in the collection of some of the data
with regard to the buildings on different streets;
Mr. E. T. Foulkes, in preparing the draft maps;
and Mr. W. W. Rockwell, in making the index.

A word may be said about the district maps.
The three having certain characteristics of the
streets indicated by colored strips are intended
to be accurate as to the prevailing condition in
each block. In the first, apartment houses are
distinguished from tenement houses as usually
having more than four rooms to a suite, with special provision for privacy and comfort. In the
map showing racial grouping, where a street is
bordered with a strip of two colors, the indication

is that no single nationality is in a majority, but that two nationalities are present each to the extent of from thirty to fifty per cent of the whole. In this case the color next the street stands for the predominant factor. In the map showing industrial grades, the two mixed colors, purple and orange, indicate the blending of a lower and a higher grade of labor, in proportions of from twenty-five to fifty per cent each. These mixed colors may, in fact, be taken to represent separate economic gradations. In the map showing institutions and meeting-places, the different symbols are to make reference to the map easy from each of the different chapters in which the different sorts of established local centres are discussed.

The data for the first and fourth of the district maps were obtained entirely by personal investigation. For the second the data were secured from the Tenement House Census giving nationality by precincts, from the State Census of 1895 giving nationality and parent nativity by wards, from the City Assessors' List for 1898 giving the names of all adult males by streets, and from considerable personal investigation. The third district map is based upon a classification of the occupations of all male adults as given by streets for each individual in the Assessors' List. The

diagram presenting the relative proportion of the
different nationalities is based on the State Census
returns just mentioned, which show the native
country of the parents of all inhabitants, thus indicating the character of the population for two
generations. The figures upon which this diagram
is based refer to Wards 7 and 9, whose population
is practically identical with that covered by the
district maps. The plan of "Two Blind Alleys"
is taken by permission from a pamphlet entitled
"Some Slums in Boston," which was prepared for
the Twentieth Century Club by Harold K. Esta-
brook, a former resident of the South End House.

In the course of the present investigation much
valuable material has been brought to light which
is available for the North and West Ends of Boston as well as for the South End. Considerable
personal examination has already been made by
residents of the South End House into the conditions of those districts. A second volume is to be
prepared, confining itself to that situation. It is
hoped also that the study may further develop so
as to embrace sketches of the outlying working-
class districts, whose problems are less complicated, and a concluding investigation of certain
greater affairs of the city, which, aside from questions of locality, have a marked bearing upon the
welfare of the working classes.

# CONTENTS

# ILLUSTRATIONS

# THE CITY WILDERNESS

## THE SOUTH END

### CHAPTER I

#### INTRODUCTORY

ISOLATED and congested working-class quarters,
with all the dangers to moral and material well-
being that they present, grow along with the
growth of all our great cities.

The course of their evolution is in nearly all
cases much the same. At first the well-to-do and
the poor live near together, the poor having their
abode on the back streets. There is no absolute
line of demarcation between the interests of the
two classes. Both share, to a degree, in a common
life. But as time goes on, the poor increase to
such an extent, through industrial change at home
and immigration from abroad, that they become
overcrowded where they are, and begin to emerge
into some of the front streets, dislodging and
pushing along their more prosperous neighbors.

Residences get into the hands of lodging-house keepers. Later, in many cases, they undergo a few alterations and become tenements. New buildings soon begin to spring up in nooks and corners of unoccupied land. Shops and other places of business line the main streets more and more. Each later immigration adds to the local population that is already taxing the housing accommodation. Factories begin to come into those parts, increasing the crowd and making the conditions still more complicated.

Meanwhile the well-to-do, establishing themselves elsewhere, have opened up centres of civilizing influence in which the working people have no share. The ties which for a time bound them to their former homes and neighbors have been severed one by one. Although perhaps owning property or interested in business at that section of the city, they have practically forgotten it in all its social and moral aspects. Cut off as it now is in great measure from the centres of the city's life, such a quarter provides fit haunts for the depraved and vicious. Evils of all kinds find here a congenial soil and produce a rank growth. The back streets, at best, are dreary and depressing, and have dark squalid courts and alleys running in from them. The chief thoroughfares gradually take on aspects of garish picturesqueness, which, set against a mixed background of poverty and moral tragedy, give them a weird fascination.

These various conditions tend to disintegrate neighborhood life and to destroy what is best in the life of the home. Neighborhoods come to be made up of people who have no local attachments and are separated from one another by distinctions of race and religion. There is no concerted action for a better social life, no watchfulness over common interests. Such a state of things gives political corruption its best opportunity. This is precisely the place where money is to be laid out at election time.

Of the several great quarters in Boston where the less prosperous dwell, the South End shows the questionable results of the city's growth the most clearly. The North End and the West End bear a certain resemblance to it. The rest — Charlestown, East Boston, South Boston, Lower Roxbury — are given over almost uniformly to middle-class and working-class homes. They have relatively little of the characteristic impress of the great city upon them. They are all at a distance from the commercial centre. Three of them are separated from it by water, and, save for their water-side industries, might imaginably exist apart from the city altogether. But both the North End and the West End, in spite of the resemblance, also present important points of difference. The West End is at the outer extreme of the city in its direction, as also is the North End, save for two of the outlying sections just mentioned; while the South End is at the city's centre of population. There are two highways to Cambridge running through the West End, and the ferry traffic to East Boston passes through the North End. The South End has no less than eight great thoroughfares crossing one another and connecting distant parts of the metropolitan area. With these go an important manufacturing region, thronged centres of amusement, and a complex population, racially and industrially, — such as do not exist in the other quarters. The North and West Ends are both hemmed in between the business section of the city and the water of the Charles River and the harbor; and the North End, lying as it does immediately between the two union railroad stations, is slowly shrinking under the encroachments of trade. In the southern direction only could a great metropolitan working-class quarter find room for its development.

This volume deals with all of that development

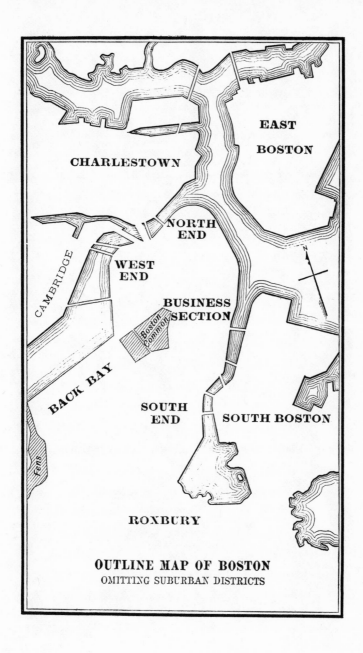

OUTLINE MAP OF BOSTON
OMITTING SUBURBAN DISTRICTS

which has as yet taken place. The district particularly to be described constitutes the inner characteristic half of the South End. The territory has
an area of not more than half a square mile, being
almost exactly a mile in length and averaging
half a mile in width. It is bounded on the northern side by Eliot and Kneeland Streets, which
together form the busy highway between Park
Square and the new Southern Union Station, and
divide the South End from the business section.
On the east is a line of wharves fringing the wa-
ters of Fort Point Channel and the South Bay,
an inlet from the harbor, over which go several
bridges to South Boston. To the south and west
the district is separated from the rest of the South
End by clearly defined bounds. With Tremont
and Ferdinand Streets on the west, and the Brookline streets on the south, begin neighborhoods
which still contain many family residences and are
altogether free, as yet, from tenement houses.

The residential section stretching beyond this
district on the Tremont Street side shows a gradually ascending social scale, from the lodging-houses
of the better class just over the border of the district to the elegant private dwellings and imposing
apartment structures of the Back Bay, where the
city's wealth and fashion have made their home.

In the section south of the district are to be seen, in the laying out of the streets and in the architecture, many evidences of what the best of the South End was like in the days when this part of the city was a prosperous residential quarter. Several of the squares here — though almost entirely deserted by their old residents — are still outwardly as pleasant places of abode as can be found within the main city. Farther on is Roxbury, with its constantly increasing number of artisans and tradespeople, together with the beginnings, in that direction, of the suburban population.

Though the district in question is thus distinctly set off by itself, it is so close to the chief centres of the city that its isolation has been rather that resulting from lack of sympathy and interest than from lack of intercommunication. Even its churches and theatres have never been merely local affairs. Its central situation and its accessibility bring in and out of it an increasing number of business men who are involved in its manufacturing and transportation interests. The higher grade of workman engaged in its industries may wish to have his family elsewhere, as the facilities of the district for transit so easily allow; but he naturally returns to this pivotal point for any business connected with the interests of his trade throughout the city. The nearness of the district to the city's throng, together with remoteness from its best life, allows an irresponsible class of people to come and go, who throw aside the ordinary restraints and give the reins to their worst impulses.

Happily, however, these channels of easy intercommunication have of recent years come to be heavily freighted with a return of sympathy and interest. In the evolution of the crowded city quarter which was traced at the beginning of this chapter, two periods only were described: that when the well-to-do and poor live in the same neighborhoods and their interests were in a measure bound together, and that marked by the more or less complete separation of these two classes and the abandonment of the poor to their fate. A third stage has been reached in not a few instances, brought about by a quickened social conscience among the well-to-do and cultured. Through a growing feeling of obligation on the part of those that have towards those that have not, attention has been directed with real concern to the city's social and moral wastes. As a result, charities and philanthropies have begun to invade them in growing number and variety. Such churches as are located there feel the reaction, and begin to take on new forms of activity the better to meet the situation presented by their respective neighborhoods; and other churches from without see in wholly neglected neighborhoods the fields for new missionary enterprise.

The South End has entered upon this stage of social recovery. There is a constantly increasing number of people in other parts of Boston and in the suburbs who are making substantial contributions of money or effort in connection with its varied centres of human service.

If any comparison were to be instituted between this and similarly conditioned districts in other cities, it would be important to remember that while this district is afflicted with all the evils that go with such situations, yet in this case those evils do not exist at their fullest stage of development. There is no such overcrowding as there is in lower New York; poverty has no such painful and revolting aspects as are to be seen in East London; drunkenness is of a less sodden and brutalizing character than in the corresponding quarters of many American cities; immorality is at least not obtrusive and defiant; and, amid a cosmopolitan population, representing nearly every grade of working-class existence, the labor problem is at about its average degree of difficulty.

There are many reasons for this comparatively moderate state of things. Boston is not a city of the first magnitude, and should not expect the extreme results of rapid growth. Though it has a compact urban population of half a million within the city limits, and half a million without, it still retains much of its old-time town feeling, which has as an accompaniment an intense sense of local responsibility. The city as a whole has the inheritance of generations of effectively organized relief and mission work. The educational system, though in some respects not so preëminent as formerly, exerts extraordinary force. It will also be remembered that public spirit in Massachusetts has embodied itself in much humane legislation for the protection of working people.

This somewhat more mature stage of progress has its risks. The sense of urgency is weakened. Attention is likely to be magnetized by the detailed manifestations of evils rather than determinedly directed toward their hidden sources. Mere executive impulse is often relied upon for what can come only of a high enthusiasm and a daily refreshed purpose.

# CHAPTER II

## HISTORICAL

JOHN WINTHROP and his associates established themselves chiefly within the district now bounded by Milk, Bromfield, Tremont, and Hanover Streets, in the heart of the city. The North End was next settled. The boundary between this new section and the older one, which came to be known as the South End, was the " old canal " or Mill Creek, which ran from the present Causeway Street to Haymarket Square, then through Blackstone and North Streets to North Market Street. A third division, situated to the west and north of Beacon Hill, was occupied somewhat later and became known as the West End. These names for the different sections of the town or city have been retained, but the boundaries of all but the North End have changed with the growth of the community.

In 1784 the North End contained, according to Shurtleff,[1] " about six hundred and eighty

[1] *Topographical and Historical Description of Boston.*

dwelling houses and tenements and six meeting houses. Though it had formerly been the court end of the town, even at the above-named period it had begun to lose its former prestige, and gave unquestionable evidences of decay and unpopularity."

The West End, according to the same authority, contained at the same period " one meeting house and about one hundred and seventy dwelling houses and tenements ; and, although the smallest and least populous of the divisions, was regarded then as a very pleasant and healthy part of the town, on account of its westerly situation, where it had plenty of agreeable inland breezes, and was comparatively sheltered from the easterly winds."

The South End of 1784 included what is now the centre of the business part of the city. The Old South Church takes its name from its location at the then South End of the town. Shurtleff says that this section " was by far the most extensive in point of territory of all the natural divisions of the town, being in length from the fortifications on the Neck to the Mill Bridge. . . . It contained all the public buildings except the Powder House, ten meeting houses, and about twelve hundred and fifty dwelling houses. Being the seat of business, it was the most flourishing part of the town, and contained the principal shops and warehouses."

The portion of the town situated south of the present Dover Street, containing a large part of the South End of to-day, had so few inhabitants before the Revolution that it was seldom referred to in describing it. It was usually spoken of as the "Neck Field," or the "Field towards Roxbury." The Neck was a narrow isthmus of about a mile in length, by which, down to the beginning of the present century, the "pear-shaped" peninsula of Boston was attached to the mainland. The Neck began at Beach Street, diminished to its narrowest point near Dover Street, then gradually increased in width to a point near Dedham Street, where it expanded to much greater proportions.

Drake,[1] writing in 1872, says that " within the recollection of persons now living the water has been known to stand up to the knees of horses in the season of full tides at some places in the road on the Neck. . . . At some points along the beach there was a good depth of water, and Gibben's ship-yard was located on the easterly side a short distance north of Dover Street, as early as 1722 and as late as 1777. Other portions on both sides of the Neck were bordered by marshes, more or

[1] *Old Landmarks and Historic Personages of Boston.*

less extensive, which were covered at high tide.
Wharves were built at intervals along the eastern
shore, from Beach Street to Dover Street. In
front of these wharves, dwellings and stores were
erected, facing what is now Washington Street."
Some of these wharves were so near the street
that people passing by complained that the bow-
sprits of ships unloading obstructed the street.

Travelers were once in great danger of losing
their way along the narrow causeway and its adjacent marshes. So frequent had such accidents
become that not only the town but the General
Court took action in 1723 to have the dangerous
road fenced in. The marshes were a favorite resort for birds and were much frequented by sports-
men. It is related that Sir Charles and Lady
Frankland one day narrowly escaped being shot
as they were passing over the Neck. In 1785 the
town of Roxbury was obliged to place sentinels
there to prevent the desecration of the Sabbath.

Till 1786, when the Charlestown Bridge was
completed, the only entrance for carriages into the
town was over the Neck. Consequently measures
were taken very early for paving it, and protecting
it from the violence of the sea. In 1708 the town
made a grant of all the land between Castle
Street and a point a little north of Dover Street

on condition that the grantees completed the highway and erected barriers " to secure and keep off the sea." In 1785 another grant was made for a similar purpose to Stephen Gore, John Way, and others, of a tract of lands and flats bounded on the south by the present Malden Street and on the north by Dover Street. This land was divided by the highway in a diagonal fashion. That the estates might present right angles to the street, a bend was made in the highway, which may be noticed in the portion of Washington Street between Dover and Malden Streets. This bend marks the high-water line on the easterly side of the Neck. A dike was built on the same side across the marshes to the mainland in Roxbury. About the same time, too, a sea-wall was built on the west side from Dover Street to a point very near to Waltham Street. Traces of this sea-wall were to be seen as late as 1868.

The early settlers found the Neck fairly well wooded; and from time to time, after the roadway was laid out, trees were planted on the sides of the highway. A view of the South End and of the Neck in 1764, which is reproduced by Shurtleff, gives a very good idea of the appearance of the present South End before the great transformations of the last seventy-five years.

In 1784, according to the account of Shurtleff, there were no buildings beyond the fortifications except a few stores. Ten years later there were only eighteen buildings between Dover Street and the Roxbury line. Drake says that "in 1800 there were not more than one or two houses from the site of the Cathedral to Roxbury. The few buildings standing between the American and British lines were burnt during the siege, and only two barns and three small houses were then left on what was properly termed the Neck."

Naturally enough, the defenses of the town early engaged the attention of the people. Although the Indians of the vicinity were regarded as friendly, they were not fully trusted, and a guard of an officer and six men was placed on the Neck in April, 1631. Probably before 1640 a small fortification was built a little to the south of Dover Street. Regular watches were kept, and at night the gates were closed and no one allowed to enter or leave the town.

This early fortification had fallen into decay before 1710, and in that year the town voted to have a new fort erected upon the same site. A substantial structure of brick and stone was accordingly built. In 1860 workmen engaged in digging for a drain in the neighborhood discovered parts of the foundations.

The third fortification was constructed in 1774 by General Gage. He strengthened the works near Dover Street and dug a deep moat, into which the water flowed at high tide. This fort was known as the " Green Store Battery " from the green-painted warehouse of " Deacon " Brown, which stood on the site of the present Grand Theatre. A stronger fortification was built near the present Canton Street. On the eastern side of the isthmus, there was also a smaller fort, between the larger ones. Where Franklin and Blackstone Squares now are, the roadway was commanded by pieces of artillery.

The British occupied for a time the farmhouse of a man named Brown, which stood on the west side of Washington Street a little south of Blackstone Square, until it was burned in July, 1775, by a raiding party of Americans. The American advanced post was at the George Tavern, which was located near the present site of the Washington Market. The tavern was burned by the British about a fortnight after the burning of Brown's house by the Americans. The Americans did not erect any fortifications on the Neck until after the Battle of Bunker Hill, when the famous " Roxbury lines " were laid out on the line between Roxbury and Boston. Later, earthworks were erected near the George Tavern and within musket-shot of the British advance guards. Tradition declares that to this point it was Washington's daily custom to come, accompanied by his personal staff of men afterwards famous in the Revolutionary War. After the evacuation of Boston, Washington sent five hundred men to enter the town under the command of one of his colonels, who unbarred and opened the gates of the British works. He himself entered the following day. On account of the smallpox, which then prevailed in Boston, the army did not come in until after several days. With the end of the siege, the usefulness of the fortifications upon the Neck ceased, and they were demolished by Washington's orders.

In October, 1786, an act was passed by the State of Massachusetts to establish a mint for the coinage of copper, silver, and gold. A master was appointed in May, 1787, and was authorized to erect the necessary buildings and to purchase machinery. The sum of $70,000 in cents and half cents was ordered to be struck as soon as possible. The works were placed on the Neck near what is now Rollins Street, and at Dedham. The copper was first taken to Dedham, where it was rolled, and then brought back to Boston to be coined.

The copper coins ordered began to be issued early
in 1788, but only a few thousand were ever circulated because of the adoption of the Federal
Constitution, which limited the right of coinage to
the general government.

A characteristic institution of the Neck was the
gallows, which was first placed on the easterly side
near the old fortifications.   Later it was removed
to a point not far from the present site of the Con-
servatory of Music, formerly the St. James Hotel.
Capital punishment was an open spectacle there
until the building of the Leverett Street Jail, about
1822, when, in accordance with the changed views
in regard to such matters, hangings ceased to be
public.

There were brickyards on both sides of Dover
Street before the Revolution.   These gave employment to many poor people during the troubled
times preceding the Declaration of Independence.
The scarcity of building stone on the site of old
Boston gave occasion for the development of this
early industry.

As has been already pointed out, the old South
End included what is now the heart of the business part of Boston.   With the growth of the
town, the South End has gradually changed its
boundaries.   Its limits have moved steadily south-

ward. Winter Street, and then Boylston Street, became the boundary. Drake says that when the Boylston Market was built, in 1810, it was considered far out of town. Near by, there was a popular tavern which had been a customary halting-place for country people who came to town with their produce. At a later period Dover Street for a time came to be regarded as the dividing line between the central part of the city and the South End.

This last boundary was set because at that point had begun the construction of a large area of "made land," reclaimed from marshes and flats by the widening of the Neck. "At the March meeting in 1800," according to Shurtleff, "the question of laying out the Neck Lands came up, and the subject was referred to the selectmen, who reported in March, 1801, presenting a plan, in which the land was divided into streets and lots, the streets being regular and drawn at right angles; and to introduce variety a large circular place was left to be ornamented with trees, which the committee said would add to the beauty of the town at large and be particularly advantageous to the inhabitants of this part, the Neck. The 'circular place' was called Columbia Square; and in reality was an oval grass plot, bounded by four streets, with

Washington Street running through its centre, — indeed, the identical territory now included in Blackstone and Franklin Squares." The old Columbia Square was for many years neglected, and was finally in 1849 divided into the two squares of the present day.

When the widening of the Neck began, there was only one street, then called Orange Street, running south from Castle Street. The South Cove extended from Beach Street, which took its name from the fact that it really formed the beach of this part of the Cove, to the Roxbury shore. The high-water mark of the Cove on the eastern side of the Neck followed an irregular line between what are now Washington Street and Harrison Avenue. On the west was the Back Bay, the eastern border of which made a concave curve running across the present locations of Tremont Street and Shawmut Avenue, from Boylston Street to a point near West Dedham Street.

The first important enterprise for the enlargement of the limits of Boston by making new land was the so-called "Front Street Improvement." The Front Street Company was chartered in March, 1804, and was composed mainly of persons owning real estate bordering on the water east of Washington Street and south of Beach Street.

The improvement consisted of the construction of a street parallel with Washington Street from Beach Street as far as the present Dover Street Bridge. This street was begun in May, 1804, and completed in October, 1805. It was named Front Street at first, but in 1841 the name was changed to Harrison Avenue, in honor of the first President Harrison. Drake says that " a straight avenue, three quarters of a mile in length and seventy feet wide, was something unknown in Boston before this street was laid out." The flats between Harrison Avenue and Washington Street were left for the owners to fill, and as late as 1830 some of them had not been filled. The cost of the improvement was about $65,000, and was paid by the owners of the land which was inclosed. About nine acres of land available for building were added to the area of the town. The agreement of the owners to build no structure less than ten feet from the street was probably the first instance in Boston of a restriction upon real estate that had in view the symmetry and general appearance of a street lined with buildings.

The great impetus to the improvement of the South End came in 1833, when the South Cove Company was incorporated with a subscribed capital of $414,500, divided into five hundred shares. It was formed as auxiliary to the Boston and Worcester Railroad, to give terminal and yard facilities. The railroad agreed to buy a large amount of land, and to establish and maintain its terminals thereon forever. The South Cove Company at first bought two million three hundred and seventy-five thousand feet of the flats, at twelve cents a foot. By 1836 it had purchased about seventy-three acres and had invested over $300,000. Material for the filling was brought chiefly in boats from the company's gravel pits in Roxbury and Dorchester, though a part was obtained in Brighton and transported by the railroad. The filling was completed in November, 1839, and in six years seventy-three acres had been added to the area of the city.

The enterprise was finally a financial success, but it saw some dark days, especially in the crisis of 1837. The company had also begun the construction of the United States Hotel, on Beach Street, and this undertaking very nearly wrecked the whole enterprise. The hotel was, when built, the largest in the country. The agent of the South Cove Company, at that time, cited as a sign of hope the fact that "the Worcester Railroad now transports about one hundred passengers daily."

The expansion of the South End began in 1805, and was not completed until the end of the sixties. The Front Street Company and the South Cove Company together filled the area from about Beach Street to Dover Street, where the town ownership began. The two companies realized about eighty acres. The remaining portion of the work was done by the town. The town filled its lands by contract, the material being taken by excavation from Fort Point Channel, the South Bay, and the gravel bank near Willow Court, Dorchester, as well as from gravel pits at a somewhat greater distance.

The widening of the Neck on the western side was accomplished as a part of the changes which finally resulted in the creation of the present Back Bay quarter as the chief residential district of the city. In 1814 the Boston and Roxbury Mill Corporation had been chartered, and given authority to build " a dam from Beacon Street at Charles to the town of Brookline (known as the Mill Dam and identical with the present line of Beacon Street), as well as a cross dam from the main dam " (on the site of Parker Street, east of the present Brookline Avenue). The company was authorized " to confine the tide within this area and the South Bay, and given perpetual flowage rights over these lands, as well as to build and operate mills by the water power obtained from the confinement of flood - tide water within the basin, and its discharge into a so-called empty basin drained at ebb tide." The company was further given power to make a roadway of each dam and levy tolls for their use. The original plan was to use as the full or flood basin the whole of the Back Bay, which then extended from the foot of the Common to the Brookline Hills, and at high tide to the Neck. The Neck was to be cut through so as to connect the Back Bay and the South Bay; and the South Bay, dammed in at the present Dover Street Bridge for the purpose of excluding the tide, was to serve as the empty basin of the system. This particular right was never made use of, either because of opposition to the building of a canal through the Neck, or from doubt as to the financial results of such an undertaking. The mill dam was finished in the early summer of 1821. Mills were soon erected to make use of the water power.

Nothing was further from the plans of the originators of the enterprise than the reclaiming of the basin for building purposes. A succession of events brought about this unlooked-for result. In 1831 the Boston and Providence and the Bos-

ton and Worcester railroads were chartered, and
their routes were projected through this territory.
In 1832 the property of the original company was
divided. A new company, the Boston Water
Power Company, took possession of the mills, the
entire water power, and all lands south of the main
dam; while the old company retained the roads
and all property north of the dam. The building
of the two railroads through the basins injured
considerably the value of the grants made; and in
addition concessions were forced from the companies by owners of adjoining property. The
final stroke, however, came from the City, which
in 1849 " declared the condition of the Back Bay
a public nuisance." Thus the filling of the whole
space became inevitable for sanitary reasons. A
State committee was appointed, and in 1852 re-
commended that the water - power interests and
mill business be abandoned, and the property be
used for land purposes. After many delays and
much conflict among the parties interested, the
basins were filled, and about five hundred acres
of valuable land added to the area of the city.

The development of the present South End by
changing a narrow isthmus into an extensive district of made land is indicated by noting the successive steps in the creation of the more important

streets and squares. As has been pointed out, there was originally only one highway over the Neck. In 1788 this received the name of Washington Street from the Roxbury line to the fortifications. In 1824 the name was extended to include the present street of the name as far as Dock Square. Harrison Avenue was the first of the streets made by filling. Albany Street, the second great thoroughfare east of Washington Street, was projected in 1839 by the South Cove Corporation southward from Beach Street, but not until 1868 did it reach Northampton Street. Of the streets on the west of Washington, the present Shawmut Avenue was first named Suffolk Street, and extended only from West Castle Street to Dover Street. This portion was made in 1836–37. It was extended from Dover Street to the Roxbury line in 1849, and through to Tremont Street in 1870. Tremont Street to a point near Pleasant Street was included in original Boston, and passed under various names during colonial and provincial times. From Frog Lane, now Boylston Street, to the corner of the present Common Street, it was in the last century successively named Clough Street, Holyoke Street, and Nassau Street. In 1824 the whole thoroughfare from Pemberton Hill to Washington Street was called Common Street, including in its course the present short cross street of that name. A little later it was altered near the junction of Pleasant Street so as no longer to reach through to Washington Street, but was extended from Pleasant Street out to the Roxbury line. It was not until near the middle of the present century that the present name was given to the entire street beginning from Scollay Square. Columbus Avenue, the third street running north and south, west of Washington Street, is almost entirely on made land from Park Square to Northampton Street, and was built between 1868 and 1871.

Of the many streets now crossing Washington Street from east to west, none existed until 1804, when a street was laid out from Orange Street to the South Bridge on Front Street, now Harrison Avenue. In 1834 this street was extended to Tremont Street and named Dover Street. Most of the cross streets south of Dover as far as the present Massachusetts Avenue, were laid out in the decade from 1826 to 1836, the impulse during these years undoubtedly coming from the activity of the South Cove Company. Many changes were made in them during the years from 1845 to 1865, along with the growth of this part of the city. Since 1870 hardly any change has occurred even in the names. The work of laying out streets since then suggests a section well occupied and undergoing only the occasional transformation due to the shifting of population.

The changes which have taken place in the South End during the past sixty years are very vividly suggested by a story told by Shurtleff about the sale of some lots situated between the present Shawmut Avenue and Tremont Street. On a rainy day in November, 1830, a literary gentleman, a resident of Roxbury, was taking his usual ride to his country home, when his attention was attracted, a short distance north of the Roxbury line, by a group of people clustered around a well known auctioneer of the time. Stopping to investigate, he found that a land sale was going on, and joining in the bidding he became the purchaser of a little over three and three quarters acres of marsh land for $269.80, " or a little over one and one half mills per square foot, for land now assessed at $1.50 per square foot, or about one thousand times its then cost." . . . Another writer,[1] referring to conditions in 1843, says : " South of Dover Street there were a few houses only. Tremont Street was a mere road, raised but little above the marsh, and for most of the way

[1] Dr. Benjamin Cotting, *Personal Reminiscences.*

with only one house on it. It was lighted as other
roads were, with oil lamps, few and far between;
and the lighting of 'the Neck' with gas, years
later, was a notable event." An old conundrum
belongs to these days when the Neck still retained
some of the characteristics of a narrow isthmus
connecting Boston with the mainland. It was as
follows: — " Why is the Roxbury omnibus like a
lady's shawl? Because it goes over the Neck and
back."

A century ago the residence section *par excel-
lence* of Boston was at the North End; as well as
upon or near Beacon Hill, where many of the old
families have always remained. Soon there began
to be a tendency away from the North End toward
the Fort Hill and Pearl Street district. " Fifty
years gone by," says Drake, writing in 1872,
" Summer Street was, beyond dispute, the most
beautiful avenue in Boston." There stood the
gardens or mansions of the old merchants or
statesmen, some of whose estates included orchards
and pasture land.

About the middle of the century, when business
began to encroach upon this neighborhood, there
was considerable uncertainty about the probable
location of a new residential section. Some predicted that South Boston would become the fash-

ionable part of the city. A writer in the Boston
Almanac for 1853 declared that " South Boston
from present appearances is predestined to be the
magnificent section of the city in respect to costly
residences, fashionable society, and the influence
of wealth." The same article stated that there
was a " process going on at the south part of the
city, of raising the streets and squares, by bringing
gravel from the country, that is destined to mod-
ify a large tract of ground, in its general appearance. The land thus raised is of a far higher
quality for building lots than such as has been elevated to a proper level by salt marsh mud."

This last fact, coupled with the development of
the street railroad at the opportune moment, determined the location of the new residential section of the period from 1855 to 1870 at the South
End. The Metropolitan Railroad procured its
charter in 1853, and opened its line from Scollay
Square to the South End and Roxbury late in
1856.

For the next fifteen years, the South End was
the growing and popular quarter of the city.
Street after street was built up with rows of the
" swell-front " brick houses, which are still the
dominant feature of the architecture of the district. Union Park and Chester Park, Franklin,

Worcester, and Rutland Squares, with many in-
tervening streets, were the chosen homes of the
prosperous.

About 1870 the filling of land in the present
Back Bay region led to the beginning of the
transfer of the residential district from the South
End to that section. This transfer was possibly
hastened somewhat by the encroachment of business, just as the earlier emigration from the Fort
Hill district to the South End had been. The
change, once begun, went on with increasing rapid-
ity as more land became available, and as fashion
pointed more and more definitely in that direction.
The South End now stands deprived of all the
elements which it possessed in its brighter days.
The profound social change which has come over
it has made the streets on either side of Dover
Street practically identical in character ; so that
the term South End now reaches back in its application almost to the old boundary at Boylston
Street.

The history of the South End is almost devoid
of dramatic incident or picturesqueness. There
are few old houses, few relics of Boston's early and
heroic past. Nowhere, as in the North End, is the
poverty lightened by bits of color drawn from historic survivals from colonial and provincial days.

Students of old Boston have found little in the district that is of any significance. Not much has therefore been written about it, and any account of it must necessarily be lacking in the elements of interest which are found in the landmarks of the original Puritan town.

MAP ILLUSTRATING THE NATURE OF THE
**LAND AND VARIOUS TYPES OF BUILDINGS**
IN A PART OF THE SOUTH END BOSTON

C. J. Peters & Son, Engrs., Boston.

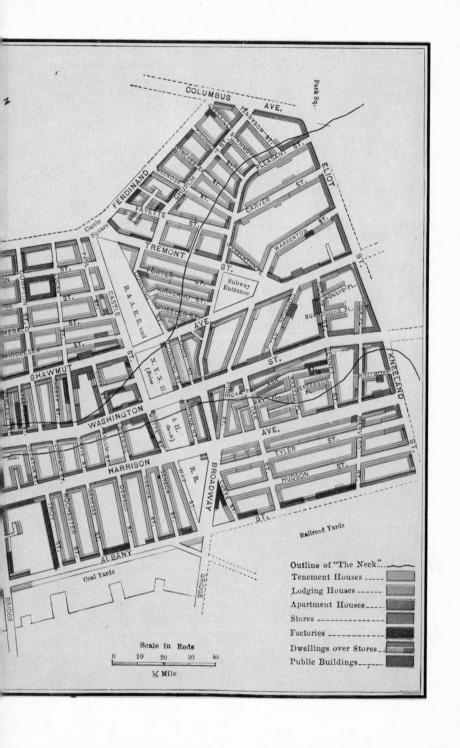

Outline of "The Neck"......
Tenement Houses ......
Lodging Houses ------
Apartment Houses......
Stores ------------
Factories ------------
Dwellings over Stores...
Public Buildings......

Scale in Rods

0    10    20    30    40

⅛ Mile

# CHAPTER III

## POPULATION

ACCORDING to the State census of 1895 the section of the South End with which this volume particularly has to do contains 40,406 inhabitants. The greater part of this population live in tenement houses. The residential portion of the district includes only about three quarters of the street space; the remainder is practically given up to trade and manufacture. Of the residential frontage one half is taken up by tenement houses and about one eighth by apartment houses. The remaining fraction is given over to lodging houses. The lodging-house region, which is one of the distinctive marks of the South End, is a natural result of the changes which have occurred in the population. The lodging houses, and many of the tenement houses also, were the private residences that were owned and occupied by prosperous American families. As the character of the population changed, and the wealthy people left the South End, their old residences, which were much too fine to be used as single dwellings for the poorer classes and not suitable for apartments, were almost of necessity turned into lodging houses. Later, as the houses became old or the neighborhood unattractive, they underwent a second transformation by being broken up into very inconvenient tenements. It being possible in this form to rent the houses in sections, they endure to a prolonged if not a useful old age.

The northern part of this district, around Hudson and Tyler Streets, contains the oldest of these houses, and consequently those which have passed through all the stages. The houses here are brick buildings from three to four stories in height, whose imposing exteriors in no way suggest the transformation which has taken place within. Some of the tenements are almost grotesque in their appearance, especially those on the first floor. For instance, in a tenement on Albany Street the kitchen and principal bedroom are connected with large sliding doors. The woodwork in both rooms is painted white. Centre pieces for chandeliers are noticeable upon the ceilings. The marble mantel which surrounds an imitation fireplace contrasts oddly enough with the small cook-stove beneath it.

The houses of this class in the southern part of

the district are larger and finer in appearance, and very few have been changed into tenement houses. This is the chief lodging-house section. A few scattered houses are still retained by the original owners for their exclusive use. The majority of families with houses to themselves are tenants, and even though they have no idea of keeping a lodging house, usually let some extra room to friends to " help out with the rent," thus doing their share in making the custom of sub-letting quite general. The lodger is by no means confined to the lodging house proper or to the private house, but fills up the extra room or two of the apartment or forces an entrance into the already overcrowded tenement. Hence lodgers are likely to be found in dwellings of all kinds : from an immense lodging house containing thirty rooms, which stands in the southern part of the district, to a little tumble-down tenement of three rooms in the northern part. This tenement was occupied by a woman with three children. Finding the third room superfluous, she sublet it to a man and his three children for a sleeping-apartment, — although the room is dark, having no outside window, and is not over eight feet square.

Not all of the tenement houses, by any means, originated from private houses. Some of the smaller streets and alleys contain houses which were apparently designed for tenements; and on a few of the streets rows of tall tenement structures have been built. Some of the apartment houses are also really nothing more than tenement houses.

This variety in the matter of dwellings is equaled if not surpassed by the variety of the inhabitants. This South End, which once rose out of the water, as it were, to become a refuge for the older American families, has now become a common resort for all nationalities. The schools reflect the situation. In the Franklin School every European country except Greece is represented; and in the Quincy School even this deficiency is made up. In this wide variety, however, a comparatively small number of nationalities makes up the greater part of the population. The Irish, Jews, British Americans, Americans, and Negroes are its chief constituents; but the English, Germans, Scotch, French, Swedes, Norwegians, Italians, Greeks, Armenians, Austrians, and a few other nationalities, are represented, though in considerably smaller numbers. And if we add to these Chinatown and the Syrian settlement in Oliver Place, both on the outskirts of the district, we supply an appropriate finishing touch to the group, — a population as complicated as it is inharmonious.

The public schools may be taken as a fair index of the distribution of the population, although the British Americans and several of the less important nationalities are not proportionately represented by the children. The parentage of the 685 children in the Franklin School shows that 200 are Irish, 170 are Americans, 121 Jews, 61 colored, 9 Germans, and 124 are of other nationalities. In the Wait School on Shawmut Avenue 241 out of 426 scholars are Jews; of the remainder, 58 are American, 55 Irish, 18 colored, 17 German, the rest of other nationalities. It is interesting to note that five years ago there were not more than ten or fifteen per cent of Jews in this school, where now there are over fifty per cent. In the Quincy School about one third are Americans, one third Irish, and one fifth Jews. The Jews and the Irish have the largest families, and hence are best represented in the schools. The people from the British Provinces, the Italians, Greeks, and Armenians are to a large extent unmarried.

However cosmopolitan the South End may be, it is not so strikingly foreign in its population as the North End is. South End people have to some extent at least become toned down and adapted to their environment through the influence of a longer residence in this country or a closer contact with American institutions. At the North End the immigrant has remained foreign because isolation is possible there. His associates are his own countrymen. His neighbors are immigrants from other countries. He does not become American for the simple reason that the North End is not American. It is Italian, Jewish, Irish, or Portuguese; and naturally the mere contiguity of these several elements, with the least possible association among them, has not produced an American type. In the South End the process of assimilation has advanced a step. Although there is still a tendency for the nationalities to group themselves, extended isolation is no longer possible. There is a more permanent tone to the life. The older immigrants have settled down in their American homes, and their children know no other. The sifting of the competent from the incompetent is still taking place, but future progress for the most part must be made by the children. While the newly arrived immigrant manifests a certain degree of energy, the chief ambition in a district like this is merely to keep from falling in the social scale; and the exertion put forth is often all too small to accomplish it. The problem at the North End is the problem of immigration, to be solved at the ports of the United States. The problem at the South End is the internal social problem.

The population of this district has been and still is predominantly Irish, although the Jewish population is becoming a very important factor. There are not less than 6300 Irish of the first generation in the district, while the Jews that were born abroad number about 2700. The Irish have, until recent years, occupied nearly all of the tenement-house neighborhoods; and they have so far withstood the advance of other nationalities that they now at least share the tenement district with them. Some Irish are found on nearly every tenement street, and parts of the district are still solidly Irish.

The Irish are mainly immigrants of the first and second generations. They are on the whole rising in the social scale, the second generation making a better showing than the preceding one; yet instances of deterioration are not infrequent. In certain localities the second generation tends to yield to the influences of idleness and evil surroundings. This double change, which is constantly going on in society, is very noticeable among the Irish people. As compared with the Jews, they seem like a people without ancestry. Each generation stands in its own strength. Thus with the Irish people environment becomes of vital importance. Its influence upon them is not merely physical but moral as well. With the Jews, this is not true to the same degree. They have inherited a wonderful amount of moral strength; they are rather careless about the environment which they make for themselves, and its effect upon them is largely of an æsthetic rather than a moral nature. The better class of Irish, particularly in the second generation, show many admirable traits. They are ambitious, imitative, and quick-witted. The majority of the Irish, however, have not yet revealed such progressive characteristics.

The Jews, Negroes, and Italians are the most inclined to form groups by themselves, partly from necessity and partly, no doubt, from choice. The Jews have occupied a part of the Pleasant Street neighborhood for forty or fifty years. Many of them in that locality are German. About fifteen years ago they began to take possession of the New York streets; [1] and now all these streets, except Troy, together with that part of Harrison Avenue

[1] Troy, Rochester, Genesee, Oswego, Oneida, and Seneca Streets are commonly known as the New York streets.

near them, are pretty much in the hands of Russian and Polish Jews. Within the last few years the closing by the police of a large number of low resorts in the centre of this district has opened the way for another large accession of Jews. The Jew is merely waiting his opportunity. He cares neither for the reputation of the street nor the standing of his neighbors; hence those streets which were formerly of a bad character are now largely Jewish streets. We find the Jews also as neighbors of the Negroes, although they have no intercourse with them. In a few cases, Jews and Negroes occupy the same house.

It is remarkable how rapidly the Jewish population has increased within the last few years. They are now working into the upper part of Harrison Avenue and into Union Park Street. The better class of Irish families, on the other hand, are retreating toward Roxbury or, in some cases, crossing over to South Boston.

The Jews are already numerous among the clientele of our philanthropic institutions, not omitting those which are religious in character. They receive with pleasure everything which is offered, except the religious teaching. To this they seem to be entirely indifferent. " I don't care what you teach my children at your Sunday-school," said one

Jewish woman. " It won't make any difference with them." And, indeed, it does not. It seems to roll off them without making the slightest impression. One hour a week in a Sunday-school does not compare in its influence with the careful instruction they receive in their homes from the parent and the rabbi.

The Jews associate little with other nationalities, principally from the choice of the other nationalities. They live as much as possible in houses which they own, and aim to be entirely independent of others. There is a noticeable spirit of coöperation among them. They start an unfortunate brother in business, and in every way they seek the success of one another.

The occupation of the Jew is the reality of his life. He enters it heart and soul, and wits also. He has an ever present purpose, for the accomplishment of which he sacrifices much. His real success comes from the intensity of this purpose. In this respect the Jews contrast strongly with the Irish. The Irish are easy-going, jovial folk, who require a strong external support to make them succeed. This contrast is forcibly shown by the difference in the patronage of the saloons by the two nationalities. The Irish are apt to make their occupation a secondary matter. They remain idle if no man hires them ; but not so the Jew. If he can get no regular employment, it is possible to gather rags and junk, and sell them. This done, he goes home and rejoices with his family in the fact that he has made twenty cents, whereas the previous day brought nothing. The Jew has a surprising power of endurance. If employed under a hard master, he still works on under conditions which would drive the Irishman to drink and the American to suicide, until finally he sees an opportunity to improve his condition. Surely the modern Jew must have been the " economic man " upon which the " dismal science " was founded.

Through its Jewish inhabitants, nevertheless, the South End has gained some advantages. One of these is in its industry, and another is in its morals. Whatever may be the external condition of the Jews, morally they are clean. Seeing that they are as moral as they are, however, it is unfortunate that they are not more so. The generosity, the warm-heartedness, and the good fellowship of the Irish again make a strong contrast with Jewish traits. We cannot dissociate the Jew from his trade, and he lacks those qualities which are most esteemed by his fellows. Morality without generosity is not likely to be admired, particularly in the South End.

The Negroes form two good-sized groups in this part of the city, — one in the Bradford Street neighborhood and the other about Porter and Kirkland Streets. The Negroes began to come into the district soon after the war, and have lived in these streets ever since. Many of the older ones were slaves, and are entirely uneducated. Nearly all the Negroes are from the South, although there are a few Nova Scotians and Cubans among them. These people exhibit nearly all grades of refinement and morality. Some of them have the instincts of gentlemen. Such deplore the behavior of their less thoughtful fellows, and, while sensitive to the insults which they so often have to bear, they have resolved to live them down through patience and endurance. The majority, however, exhibit the usual characteristics of the Negro race: loud and coarse, revealing much more of the animal qualities than of the spiritual. Yet even they are good-natured and obliging people, and are often, of course, very religious in their crude way.

There is a degraded class of Negroes which, through its unfortunate prominence, seriously injures the reputation of the whole. These are not only coarse and vulgar, but idle, vicious, and immoral. They are extremely loose in their marriage relations. Desertions are quite frequent; but they are probably not so frequent as they would be if the women did not contribute a large part of the support of the family. The women seem to be, on the whole, unconcerned over these desertions. Sometimes a woman will take such treatment as a sort of insult and assume an injured air; more often she is relieved at being "rid of him." These Negroes spend a great deal of time in drinking and quarreling; and the Kirkland Street district is visited frequently by the patrol wagon. In fact, this neighborhood is one of the worst in the South End, if not in the whole city. Idleness is of course largely responsible for this state of things. The Negroes in general encounter unusual difficulties in securing employment. They seem to be forced into some sort of personal service, for which they are so well fitted; but this fails to supply work for all. If it were not for the Dinahs who, as they say, "does washin's and ironin's," many families would be destitute.

A few Italians live in the South End, who apparently have no connection with the North End colony. Some of them have lived here ten or twelve years. There are perhaps five hundred of them in all, and most of them live on Hudson, Genesee, and Oneida Streets. They are Calabrians and Sicilians. They have three or four grocery stores of their own, and seem to live quite by themselves. They have no church and no religion. Their occupation is day labor, but they get little work and small wages.

The Greeks, who in some respects resemble the Italians, are a very friendly and courteous people. There are fifty or seventy-five of them in the district, nearly all of whom are men, from fifteen to thirty years of age. There are only a few Greek families in the city. Most of the Greeks have been in this country from three to twelve years. They are very patriotic, ready to hasten to the assistance of their country, or give money for her support; yet they are all citizens of this country, or on the way to being so, and intend to make this country their permanent home. The Greeks of this district may be industrially grouped with the Jews and Syrians into a petty merchant class; although in Lowell, where they are quite as numerous as in Boston, they are employed as factory hands.

The Syrians are nearly all peddlers, if they are anything. Some are persistent candidates for charity. There are very few of them in the South End outside of Oliver Place. Next to the Chinese, who can never be in any real sense American, they are the most foreign of all our foreigners. Whether on the street in their oriental costumes, or in their rooms gathered about the Turkish pipe, they are always apart from us. They are hospitable in their homes, but they are also deceitful; and out of all the nationalities they would be distinguished for nothing whatever excepting as curiosities.

About seventy Chinamen are scattered throughout the district following their accustomed occupation of laundering. Just beyond the inner border of the district, at the lower end of Harrison Avenue, is the central Chinese colony of the city; and here trading is an important occupation. The launderers being more isolated and frequently in rather hostile surroundings, do not develop their real characteristics as do the inhabitants of Chinatown. Its stores, restaurants, and theatre are accessible to the outsider; but the darker side of Chinese life is not so easily penetrated. The horrors associated with opium smoking are, however, kept at the minimum through the constant watchfulness of the police. The Chinaman is perhaps most attractive in his capacity of Sunday-school scholar, though his responsiveness to missionary effort merely reflects his strong desire for some knowledge of the vernacular.

Among the other nationalities of the northern

part of the district should be mentioned the one hundred and twenty-five Armenians who are scattered throughout the various lodging houses of that section. Like the Greeks, the Armenians are nearly all young men. The greater part of them have come to America within the last three years as a result of the Turkish atrocities. Not all of the Armenian residents in the district are permanently settled. The Armenians and Greeks learn our language much more readily than the Italians, partly because their occupations demand it more, and partly because they are not so illiterate as the Italians. The section of the city around Kneeland and Beach Streets is now a centre for the three hundred Armenians in the city. Three or four Armenian restaurants in that vicinity have become their social meeting-place. Most if not all of the refugees have by this time found employment, some in families, and some in factories. Their purpose is to give assistance as soon as possible to their relatives in need.

When we turn from the tenement houses to the lodging houses, we find a marked change in the character of the inhabitants. Although there is here a great diversity of nationalities, we find a much more homogeneous whole. The South End lodgers are hard to analyze. They really comprise those of the working classes who are single, with a few married couples who have not yet made themselves homes; that is, they stand for the large number of unmarried persons who have come to Boston from a distance to make their fortunes — and have not yet made them. The lodging house reveals to a considerable extent the great movement of young people from the country to the city, and the immigration of unattached persons from other countries. Almost as many nationalities are included among the lodgers as are found in the district, yet the better lodging houses are filled principally with Americans and British Americans, and a lesser number of English and Irish. The lodgers are not really characterized by nationality, however, but rather by their mode of life; for the stamp of the lodging house finally overshadows that of nationality.

The British Americans are principally from the Maritime Provinces. Not including a few French Canadians they number 3500. They are Scotch and Scotch-Irish, with a few English among them. Nova Scotia sends the greatest number, and New Brunswick the next. Others come from Prince Edward's Island and Newfoundland. The Nova Scotians seem to be the most desirable. They are of fair intelligence and very industrious. The people from Prince Edward's Island, on the other hand, are quite likely to be illiterate and are generally of a somewhat inferior type. The men from the Provinces are usually clerks and artisans, but they do not represent much skill. Many of them reside here only during a part of the year, and do not spend their money here. A greater number of women than men come from the Provinces, but they enter domestic service so generally that probably fewer of them are found in the lodging houses than of the men.

The Americans in the lodging houses are young men from the country, principally from northern New England. The youth comes to Boston in search of larger opportunities and a broader life than the country affords. He finds hard work and small pay. Poor food in a cheap boarding house, and a cheerless room, together take most of his wages. His associates are often coarse, his amusements few, his home comforts merely those which he can himself provide. He sees life in its bald reality, and soon becomes acquainted with the vices of a great city. The lodging houses themselves are the homes of the queer and questionable of every shade. The life of the lodger is at best an uninviting and monotonous one; he is fortunate if it is not an evil one. The members of a few of the nationalities lodge with persons from their own country ; but in the majority of cases lodging-house groups are not according to national lines. Business or social interests more frequently determine such companionship.

From these people who live in single dreariness, it is a relief to turn to those who love home life, like the Germans and the Scotch. These nationalities are not largely represented in the South End. The German element is a little larger than the Scotch, which numbers only about four hundred. Both are industrious folk and make good citizens. Formerly, Germans were found here in greater numbers than they are now. The bulk of them are in a colony in Roxbury, where they are employed in the breweries. Such as remain are bakers, small storekeepers, or artisans. Most of them are clustered together in a little neighborhood which is a religious and social centre for many Germans throughout the city. They stand at the edge of the middle class. There are none of the very poor among them.

There are more English in the district than one would at first imagine, — about one thousand in all, — but they are not conspicuous among the mass. They form a rather more skilled class of workmen than those who come from the Provinces.

They are of course easily assimilated, and they would soon become indistinguishable among the Americans themselves if it were not that they are rather loath to lose their English character.

Of Americans there are really three types in the district. Besides the lodging-house class, there are those who have had a successful life in the South End, but retain their homes from choice; and the class of retrograding Americans, those who through incompetency or misfortune are slowly drifting downward. Neither of these classes is very large, but together they represent all that is left of the " old American " population.

The settlement and growth of this district took place principally during the first half of the present century. During the second half has occurred the transformation in the character of the inhabitants. In 1825 the district contained about 8000 inhabitants, having increased 83 per cent in five years. This was a period of marked development for the whole city. By 1840 the population had become 14,152. From 1840 to 1845 was another period of very rapid growth. The local population increased to 21,924, a gain of 76 per cent, while the population of the city as a whole increased but 34 per cent in the same time. Only 4783 inhabitants were then reported as living

south of Dover Street.[1]   The section north of
Pleasant Street showed the greatest gain, having
increased 88.8 per cent, a large part of this being
due, according to Mr. Shattuck, to the increase in
the foreign population.  The South Cove was settled during that period, and added its quota to the
growing number of inhabitants.

The population of the district at this time was
mainly American ;  the foreign element, that is,
the foreign born and their children, comprising
only 29 per cent of the whole.  The American
population was not, however, composed principally
of native Bostonians, but of Americans born in
other parts of the United States.   This class
amounted to 41 per cent of the whole, — which
was about the same proportion as existed in the
city at large, and is a much larger proportion than
is found in the city at the present time.

Nearly all of the foreign population was located
in the northern part of the district; the section
south of Dover Street was still not thickly settled.
It is related that in 1849 an Irishman who established himself on Brookline Street in the good
old Irish way, keeping a pig and chickens in his
little yard, was such a novelty in the neighborhood

[1] See the census of Boston taken in 1845 by Mr. Lemuel
Shattuck.

that the school children used to make a pastime of "going to see the Irishman." A few years after this, however, "seeing an Irishman" became no longer a pastime, and the Americans became anxious to take their recreation in some other way.

The large Irish immigration into Boston following the Irish famine of 1846 caused a general redistribution of the population. The Irish filled up the South Cove and Fort Hill neighborhoods, and the American inhabitants of these sections began to take refuge in the West End and particularly in the new houses at the South End. Since 1845 the increase in numbers has been confined to the southern part of the district, for the section north of Pleasant Street contained an even greater number of inhabitants then than now. The growth of the foreign elements in the southern section has been gradual but persistent.

In 1855 there were about 8000 foreigners in the district, two thirds of whom were Irish. The German element, a part of which were Jews, was the next largest. There were about 1100 of them, forming the largest proportion of Germans that the district has ever contained. There was a scattering number of English and British Americans. Other foreign nationalities were represented in very small numbers.

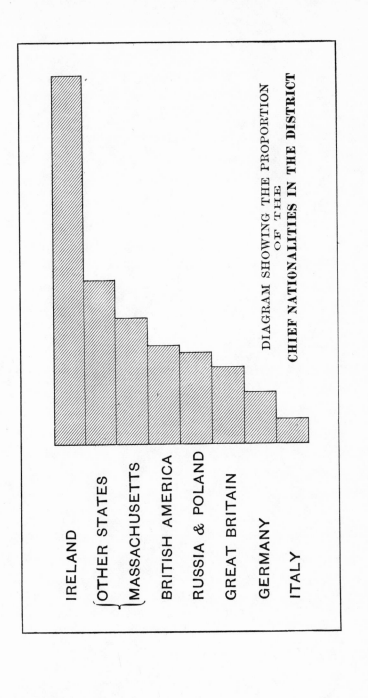

DIAGRAM SHOWING THE PROPORTION OF THE
CHIEF NATIONALITIES IN THE DISTRICT

IRELAND

{ OTHER STATES
MASSACHUSETTS

BRITISH AMERICA

RUSSIA & POLAND

GREAT BRITAIN

GERMANY

ITALY

Since this time the Irish have not increased so rapidly as other nationalities, although the leveling of Fort Hill in 1867 turned a considerable number of them into the South End. After the streets of the Back Bay were opened and the social decline of the South End began, the change of private residences into lodging houses was accompanied by an increase in the proportion of certain nationalities, especially the British Americans. By 1870 the British Americans had become the second largest of the foreign nationalities, which position they continue to hold. Americans that are not natives of Boston have increased steadily in numbers, but their relative proportion has diminished, owing to the more rapid increase of the foreign elements. In 1875 this class and the foreign born represented each about one third of the population. In 1895 of the persons born outside of Boston native Americans comprise about one fourth of the local inhabitants, and the foreign born about five twelfths.

The actual native or foreign character of the district, however, is more closely come at through the returns for " parent nativity," [1] which associate each person with his racial identity rather than his

[1] Furnished in special detail from the State census for 1895 by the *Massachusetts Bureau of Statistics of Labor.*

birthplace. Estimates based on these show that there are 5770 persons whose parents were born in Massachusetts, and 6283 whose parents were natives of other parts of the United States; making the entire element that has been American for at least two generations thirty per cent of the population. Of the foreign factors, the Irish — first and second generation — alone form thirty-two per cent of the inhabitants. The number of British Americans is not materially changed by reckoning the parent nativity. They constitute about nine per cent of all. Combining the Russian and Polish totals and adding one half of the German element as the probable share of Jews of that nationality, we have over eleven per cent as the Jewish proportion. The British have nearly six per cent. The Italians and all the Germans constitute but 1.7 per cent and 2.5 per cent respectively; the Italians being on the increase in the district and the Germans not. Austrians, French, and Swedes have the lead in the varied remainder.

The most noticeable change of population after the district became thickly settled was in the decrease of the American inhabitants as the older foreign elements increased, — the Irish, Germans, and British Americans. The proportion which the Americans bear to the total population has

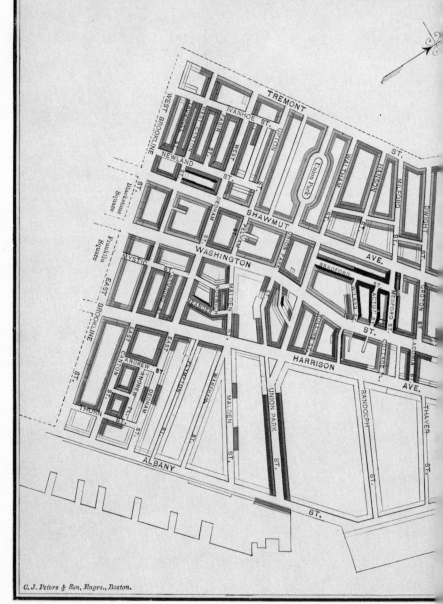

MAP ILLUSTRATING THE
**DISTRIBUTION OF THE PREDOMINANT RACE FACTORS**
IN THE POPULATION IN A PART OF THE SOUTH END BOSTON

C. J. Peters & Son, Engrs., Boston.

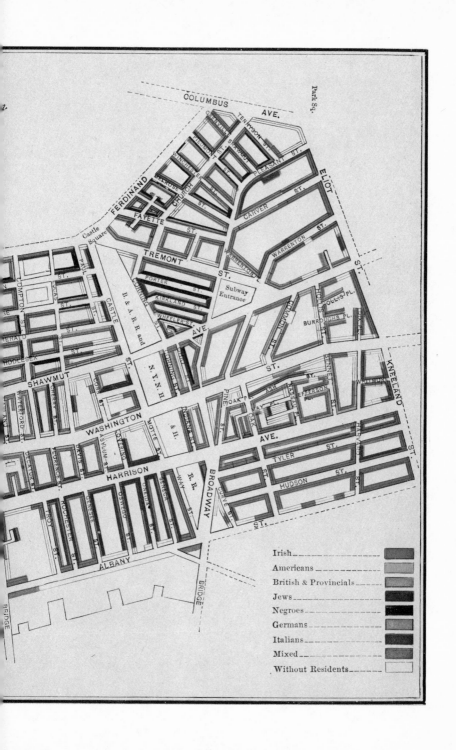

diminished forty-one per cent since 1845. The American falling off still continues, but the increase of the Irish and Germans is now confined principally to the second generation. Only one half of these elements is now composed of persons born abroad. Additions to the number of the foreign born have taken place of late chiefly among the Russian and Polish Jews and the Italians. The increase of these nationalities during the last few years makes it probable that the Irish, even including the second generation, will not long maintain their familiar predominance in the South End.

# CHAPTER IV

## PUBLIC HEALTH

DR. HOLMES has said that the training of a
child begins with its grandparents; and it is no
less true that the sanitary conditions of a given
locality, largely determining the physical, mental,
and moral trend among its inhabitants, are dependent to a great extent upon a state of things
produced by the action of preceding generations.
Setting aside any consideration of the soil or the
climate of the South End in so far as they are
the work of nature, one meets certain conditions
of earth and air, entirely of man's making, which
bear strongly upon this subject.

It has been shown that by far the greater part
of this district consists of land reclaimed from
the sea. From this fact many difficulties arise in
drainage and the erection of buildings. Much of
the land is thoroughly water-soaked but a few feet
down, as is often proved in the driving of piles for
the foundation of buildings. There was a very
recent instance of this between Harrison Avenue

and Albany Street, where the amount of water that was splashed about, as the weight fell, was so great as to make it necessary for the workmen to be clad in rubber garments. So thoroughly is the soil saturated with water that most of the basements and cellars of the district are very damp, — in many cases they are wet. During a heavy and long-continued easterly storm this condition is aggravated to such an extent that water actually oozes through old walls and floors. To give a single experience: in a front basement on the easterly side of Harrison Avenue, a woman was found lying ill upon a mattress, which lay upon the board floor; and under the floor the water could be heard to swash at every step. The soil through which such moisture has percolated is made up of no one knows what; as, in the past, material was used for filling that improved methods no longer tolerate, — the "dump" being now guarded by comparatively stringent regulations. That this is not a mere fancy was brought out during the recent extensive excavations in constructing the subway, when the stench of "made land" was an offense to the nostrils, and there was a comparatively large increase in the amount of malarial disease in the city.

Throughout this district many basements without sub-cellars are used by the very poor as dwelling places. One or two rooms, with poor ventilation, with little or no direct sunlight, with walls always damp and sometimes wet, represent to men, women, and children — home. A regulation of the Board of Health prohibits the use of a basement as a living-room unless more than one half of the abutting wall is above the adjacent street, but there is no regulation which requires that the walls and floors of basement rooms so used be waterproof. If the soil in this district were dry and sandy, with an easy natural drainage, basements conforming to the above regulation might be habitable ; but considering the soil conditions here present, such basements should certainly not be used as dwelling places.

In former years much trouble was experienced all over this district by the backing up of water through the soil pipes, on account of high tides and easterly storms, this trouble being aggravated by the fact that many sewers opened directly into the South Bay. The construction of the intercepting sewer and the enforcement of a better system of trapping have largely, though not entirely, remedied this evil. It is questionable if the difficulty can be entirely remedied. The intercepting sewer has, however, been highly successful in one respect; that is, in preventing the pollution of the South Bay, which used to be a constant menace to health and comfort.

Observation of this district extended over ten years has shown many changes, but left one crowning evil deeply impressed upon the mind, — the great overcrowding of buildings upon such areas as are not devoted to manufacture or business.[1] This overcrowding has come about in various ways. In one class of cases, the original house was built many years ago of either wood or brick. It was set well back from the street, had an attractive front yard, space on each side and at the back; and was evidently an airy, sunny residence. Now it is shut in upon all sides by blocks of dwellings, its back yard stolen away, its front yard filled up, and its once delightful approach being now down several steps and through a dark tunnel under a brick block. There sits the old house, not only without elbow room, but without breathing room; yet to several families it still passes for a home.

In another instance the overcrowding comes

---

[1] The territory between Dover Street and the railroad — including about one sixth of the district — is more compactly built with dwellings than any similar area in the city. It contains 157 persons to the acre.

about in an exactly opposite way. The houses were originally built in blocks abutting upon the street. They had in the rear a narrow street or alley for the delivery of market supplies and the gathering up of refuse, entrance to these back alleys being afforded by a passageway running in from the cross streets. Ells not originally intended have in many cases been added to these houses, and in almost every case the intersections of alleys have been used as a location for new construction, since such intersections afford a certain increased modicum of light. Moreover, in many places the original construction, which consisted mainly of three stories above a basement, has been either altered into or replaced by a building of from four to six stories. This latter sort of overcrowding occurs to a great extent in the South Cove section.[1] All over that region there are many places, alleys, and courts, in which are the homes of comparatively large numbers of people. So prominent is this form of overcrowding in that quarter that in many cases addresses are given, not at a certain street and number, but in the rear of that number. The lower parts of these courts are always damp, especially in those which have an opening toward the North. A specific instance may be cited of a

[1] East of Harrison Avenue, between Broadway and Kneeland Street.

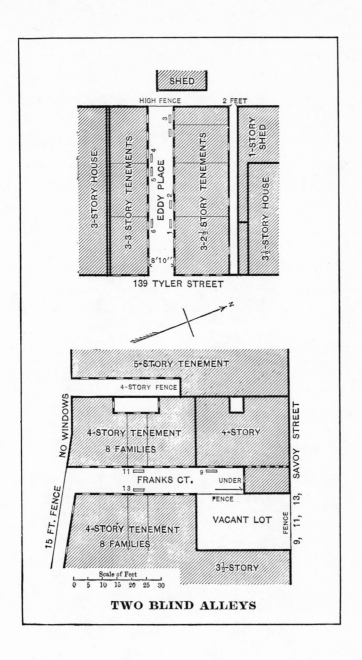

SHED

HIGH FENCE                    2 FEET

3-STORY HOUSE

3-3 STORY TENEMENTS

EDDY PLACE

3

4

5

6

1

2

8'10"

3-2½ STORY TENEMENTS

1-STORY SHED

3½-STORY HOUSE

139 TYLER STREET

Z

5-STORY TENEMENT

4-STORY FENCE

NO WINDOWS

4-STORY TENEMENT
8 FAMILIES

4-STORY

SAVOY STREET

11

FRANKS CT.

9

UNDER

13

FENCE

15 FT. FENCE

4-STORY TENEMENT
8 FAMILIES

VACANT LOT

FENCE

9, 11, 13,

3½-STORY

Scale of Feet
0  5  10  15  20  25  30

**TWO BLIND ALLEYS**

court opening off Albany Street, which has a southern exposure as far as it has any. It is surrounded by wooden buildings. The wood throughout the lower stories of the buildings is covered with green mould and is not dry even in midsummer. Higher up, where the sunlight permeates through, the clapboards are comparatively dry, and the damp, musty odor less noticeable.

There remain certain areas in which the overcrowding, due partly to both of the tendencies just described, is still more marked because in the original laying out of the town sufficient street area was not provided, nor has since been furnished. Above Dover Street, on both sides of Washington Street, this is very evident. That this section was ever " laid out " appears improbable. Alleys, courts, and places abound, though recently some of them have been rechristened streets, — a street in this case being one of a series of passageways in which no vehicle can be turned around if it be larger than a handcart. In such localities the enforcement of never so radical building laws would not relieve the condition of overcrowding, the first requisite being the addition of more street area.

The fact that the dwelling places of the district have not sufficient air space without is not their only fault. There is the additional fact that in most instances the buildings are not properly constructed for their present uses. With the exception of a few apartment houses, and fewer well-planned tenement houses, the district is made up of houses originally intended for private residences, and altered in the least degree demanded by the exigencies of the case, — by which one really means the rush to bring in the greatest rent for the smallest investment.

As far as boarding or lodging houses are concerned, the trouble is mainly with the arrangements for bathing and other sanitary purposes. The water-closets in these houses are in many instances old-fashioned and have a very scanty flushing supply. This, added to the fact that they are used by a large number of persons, makes them a menace to the health of the occupants of the house. A frequent source of difficulty, also, is that too many lodgers occupy one room.

If a family residence is more or less poorly adapted for use as a lodging house for a considerable number of people, it is entirely unfitted for use as a tenement house. The typical private house of former days has three stories above the basement; each story having two large rooms and two side rooms, or its equivalent; the front base-

ment being intended for the cellar, and the rear
basement for the kitchen. Such a house, built for
the accommodation of one family, very commonly
shelters from four to eight. A sink with running
water has been put at the head of each flight in
the hallway, or into one or both square rooms on
each floor. The water-closet arrangements have
not been changed, the one water-closet now serving
for from fifteen to thirty people. There are no
conveniences for the disposal of house offal or
ashes except the barrels in the yard. The yard
in many instances has its space taken up by a
shed. The conveniences for drying clothes are
inadequate, and there are no bathing facilities.
In this class of tenement house there is only one
redeeming feature, which is that there is no dark
room and there are no rooms opening upon a well.
The overcrowding of buildings upon the land has
lessened the breathing space of these houses, but
each room has a certain amount of direct light.

In many of the buildings which have been specially constructed for tenements, the evil of dark
rooms is very apparent. The open shafts are
often very narrow, and furnish the sole inlet of air
and light, not only for sleeping-rooms, but also
for small compartments containing water-closets ;
which, having been put in before the present strin-

gent regulations requiring ventilated traps were in force, send their contamination out into these same wells. Such a condition is manifestly insanitary, especially when it is taken into consideration that many of these shafts have roofs of glass. There are, to be sure, ventilators at the top, but they are generally kept closed.

Thus are the people of this district housed, and under such conditions are their children born and nurtured.[1] The houses, crowded upon the land, have not enough breathing space and are shut in from the sun; therefore the people have insufficient air and light, which are the first requisites for good health. Disease germs of all sorts live longest and flourish best under conditions of darkness and dampness. Sunlight and fresh air are the enemies of disease; they are by far the cheapest and most efficient disinfectants. Dampness, darkness, and poor ventilation are the most potent predisposing causes of many serious ailments that either endanger life or greatly limit its usefulness. The welfare of the community clearly demands that no person be allowed to live under such depressing conditions.

[1] The figures of the *Tenement House Census of 1891–92* show that fully one fourth of the tenement-house population of the district live under specially objectionable sanitary conditions.

The same physical results of insufficient breathing space are made worse by the overcrowding of the individuals within the houses. Such overcrowding also tends to lower the moral standards of the poor. Modesty is hardly possible when from four to ten people of varying ages and both sexes live in from two to four rooms, some of them very small. Insufficient water-closet facilities also conduce to a low standard of morals, as well as to a lessened equation of resistance to disease, owing to the difficulties in the way of the formation of regular habits. The overcrowding of tenements is an excellent reason for the late hours at which young children of the poor go to bed; it being hardly possible for the children to sleep in the midst of work and talk, until they are thoroughly exhausted. As a matter of fact, children of four and five years are often awake until nine or ten o'clock at night.

Cleanliness of body and of clothing is by these two forms of overcrowding, without and within, put at a high premium. There are practically no bathing facilities in the tenement houses of the district. That the people desire to bathe has been proved by the very large attendance at the public swimming baths during the summer season; and the new City bath-house recently opened on Dover

Street; for use all the year round, is already showing that these same people are just as anxious to
bathe during the cooler months. Outside of the in-
ability to buy many changes of underclothing, due
to poverty, the insufficient yard or shed accommodations for drying the family washing materially hinders the solution of the clean-clothes
problem. It is therefore very difficult for parents,
however well inclined, to train their children to
habits of cleanliness and neatness, or for adults
to preserve that self-respect which depends upon
the bath and fresh clothing.

To better the conditions of the poor as far as
overcrowding is concerned is entirely within the
power of the City or State. The present statute
empowers the Board of Health to condemn or
destroy buildings that are either themselves unfit
for human habitation, or render buildings in their
vicinity unfit.[1] The literal exercise of this power,
together with special legislation for the laying out
of more street area in certain portions of this district; the establishment of small public parks, not
for show but for use as playgrounds; the abolition

---

[1] The chief activity of the board in this respect has been at
the North End, where there is a number of particularly dark,
insanitary courts which, room by room, are the most congested
spots in the city.

of blind alleys; the regulation of the light and ventilation of tenement houses; more stringent rules in regard to interior sanitary arrangements; the requirement of better facilities for drying clothes — would reduce to a minimum the danger to which the community is now exposed by the advent among us of large numbers of foreigners bred to squalor, dirt, and ignorance. The evil effects of overcrowding reproduce themselves in geometrical ratio, and soon will, if they do not already, imperil the health and morals of the city's population. Such improvements, moreover, although apparently very expensive, eventually increase the rent and therefore the tax valuation of the district improved, as has been shown in many instances; and, what deserves special emphasis, they are of all means for the bettering of the poor the most clearly within the province of the government, and the most easily enforced.

The great change which has been wrought by legislation in the sanitary appointments of factories and mercantile establishments bears strongly upon this point. The laws protecting employees against bad air, noxious products, and the causes of accident, and providing, in the case of working-women, even for their self-respect and their comfort, are satisfactory in their terms and, so far at

least as this district is concerned, are faithfully
enforced. State legislation, also, happily leaves
it practically unnecessary to say anything about
sanitary evils involved in tenement-house industry.

Excepting light and air, the most important
factor in the life of a human being is food. How
then are our people fed? The inspection of food
stuffs of all sorts is a function of the Board of
Health, and by them is intrusted to an inspector.
Whenever a market of any sort is opened in the
city, the proprietor receives a visit from this inspector and is handed a card upon which are
printed certain extracts from the Public Stat-
utes which define the offense of selling unwholesome provisions, and prescribe the penalty for such
offense.[1] After this card has been delivered, frequent visits are made, which soon reveal to the
inspector the tendencies of the dealer. Any apparent inclination to break the law is met with a
warning, and this if it be not heeded is soon followed by prosecution.

Hucksters who sell provisions from wagons or
push-carts have first to obtain a license from the
Board of Police. They also are made aware of
the law, and its infringement is followed by loss
of license. Information received from the inspec-

[1] Chapter 58, Sections 5 and 6.

tor, and from various representative wholesale dealers and commission men, leads to the belief that little unwholesome food stuff is sold to the poor. It is frequently of second quality, — as, for instance, in the case of fish and fruit, — but is generally edible and wholesome. The poor go to a market or buy of the huckster, in either case seeing the goods. They are not easily deceived, but several circumstances are not in their favor. Being poor, they usually buy provisions of an inferior quality, because the price is low; and for the sake of convenience they often purchase at a small neighboring shop which is well known to carry goods of a lower grade than those that may be obtained a little farther away.

Baking powders and similar products are a subject of State regulation and examination. Milk and vinegar are inspected by a specially appointed official who is very active, and the quality of these staples is usually good. During the summer scientifically prepared milk of a superior quality is furnished free to sick children of the poorer people, the fund which pays for this milk being furnished by public subscription. The lives of many children are saved by this charity.

The art of cooking provisions so as to obtain from them the greatest amount of nourishment,

and render them most easily digested, is little
understood by our working classes, and will be
learned only by long training.  The instruction
in simple cooking in our public schools is a move
in this direction.  Improper feeding of young
children is everywhere prevalent among the tenement-house dwellers.  Very young children are
given fat meat, baked beans, and other strong
foods, as well as tea, coffee, and beer.  This error,
so productive of grave results, especially in the
summer season, will continue until such ignorance
is dissipated by rational hygienic instruction.

Throughout the district the streets are kept
fairly clean, and in summer are well watered.
Constant familiarity with them has seemed to reveal the fact that these streets receive as good
care as do those in more pretentious parts of the
town, for which the street cleaning division deserves hearty commendation.  Some of the narrow
streets are paved with asphaltum, which is very
desirable because it may be washed.  It is also
sufficiently economical, seeing that these streets
have little or no heavy teaming over them.  Alleys,
open and blind, such as are used for passageways
or as the only entrance to dwellings, are usually
fairly clean.  They are, however, prejudicial to
health and morality, and should not exist, — ex-

cept for access to rear yards, — in this or in any other section of the city.

The means used in Boston for preventing the spread of contagious diseases are excellent, and in this respect the Board of Health is most efficient. The law requires all physicians to report to the Board of Health any case of contagious or infectious disease, and postal cards are furnished by the city for this purpose. If, in the opinion of the Board of Health, any case of contagious disease is a menace to the public health, the person may be removed to the hospital. If the person is allowed to remain at home, — the board having decided that it is no menace to the community, — the fact of its presence must be plainly advertised by a card placed upon or near the door of the dwelling; and this card may be removed only by an officer of the Board of Health.

Whenever a case of contagious disease occurs in a house, the children in that house may not attend a public school until fourteen days after recovery, removal to the hospital, or death. The Board of Health fumigates the house after cases of smallpox, diphtheria, and scarlet fever; but it rarely does so in the milder contagious diseases, such as measles and chicken pox.

Public-school children are carefully guarded

against· contagious diseases. Vaccination is compulsory for admission to the public schools. The city is divided into small districts, each being under the care of a physician, who receives a small salary. This physician visits the public schools in his district, and examines all children who are reported ailing. All suspicious cases are sent home. If diphtheria is suspected, a culture is taken for bacteriological examination. The same physician also keeps track of all cases of contagious disease reported in his district.

The sanitary condition of schoolhouses as to ventilation and drainage is being constantly improved throughout the city, as a result of a rather vigorous crusade by public - spirited individuals. Schoolhouses should be as nearly perfect in this respect as present knowledge will permit; and it is not only the right but the duty of all citizens to demand such conditions. In fact, to submit school children to depressing influences of bad light and bad air is little short of criminal. It is to be hoped, then, that there will be no cessation of this crusade until the highest point possible is reached.

It is the duty of the Board of Health to inspect the plumbing of any house whenever one of its occupants has a grave infectious disease, such as typhoid fever; or at the request of any occupant.

Whenever such inspection shows the plumbing of a house to be defective, the Board of Health may order the owner either to repair or renew the plumbing, making it conform to certain minimum requirements laid down by law. Prosecution by the board may follow failure to comply with its instructions. In all new houses the plumbing must also be up to the maximum requirements of the board.

There are ample means of relief for dwellers in this district who are overtaken by sickness; and such means are more nearly at hand here than in any other working-class section of Boston. This condition has arisen not through any plan other than what is involved in the central location of the district. It may truthfully be said that if the poor man or his family go uncared for, in case of sickness, either it is his own fault, or it is because he is a very recent immigrant without friends and unacquainted with the language. The sources available to him are adequate as well in kind as in amount. He may enter a hospital as indoor patient; he may go there daily, or as often as is necessary, as an outdoor patient; or he may receive the care of a physician at his own home, and through the physician's good offices receive also a certain amount of nursing and of suitable food.

The Boston City Hospital, on Harrison Avenue, is just outside the district. Here all cases of acute disease and such as need surgical aid on account of accident or otherwise are admitted to the hospital, the bed capacity of the hospital being constantly increased to meet the increasing demand. Chronic cases, except those in which death is near, are not admitted to this hospital except temporarily, it being plainly the best policy to use the hospital for acute cases. The contagious wards of this hospital have recently been removed to a new location, apart from the main group of buildings, and are as good as any in the world. The accident room of the City Hospital is open day and night; and ambulances, either from the hospital stables or from certain of the police stations, are at the command of the public at all hours. The out-patient department of the City Hospital is for the relief of such persons as require but cannot afford the offices of a physician, while they do not need to be admitted to the hospital.

Near the City Hospital is the Massachusetts Homœopathic Hospital, at which those desiring homœopathic treatment may receive it either within the hospital or as out-patients.

St. Elizabeth's Hospital, on the southern edge of the district, is controlled and managed by sis-

ters of the Order of St. Francis (Roman Catholic).
Relief is afforded to all worthy applicants without
any reference to religious belief. This hospital,
especially in its out-patient departments, is very
popular among the Roman Catholics of this part
of the city. Many indoor patients are able to pay
a small sum, and prefer to do so, — the amount
paid being from three to five dollars per week.
Only women and young children are received as
indoor patients at this hospital. Some chronic
cases are admitted, and the hospital has an excellent maternity ward. In the out-patient department, both sexes are treated.

At the other end of the district there is an out-
patient department of the New England Hospital
for Women and Children, and at this department
a large number of patients are treated.

Also in the northerly portion of the district is
located the Boston Dispensary, a long-established
charitable institution for the relief of the sick
poor. A corps of physicians and surgeons are at
the dispensary every morning for the treatment of
those who are able to come there, all the special
branches of medicine and surgery being represented. In rendering such service the dispensary
is like the out-patient department of a hospital;
but another sort of relief is also available here.

The dispensary extends its ministry widely from this centre. The city is divided into sections, each one of which is under the care of a physician. Calls may be left at the dispensary or at one of its sub-stations in other parts of the city up to ten o'clock in the morning, insuring the attendance of a dispensary physician within a reasonable time, generally before noon. Each physician is attended by a nurse of the District Nursing Association who not only assists him in his offices, but is also even better able than he to carry cheer and to furnish, by example and precept, little lessons in better living to the poor with whom she comes in contact. Both the physician and the nurse coöperate with the Associated Charities in the relief of distress and want among the families of their patients. In addition the physician is able to order from one of the diet kitchens, for such of his patients as are destitute, those various sorts of cooked or uncooked food that are so grateful, if not necessary, to the sick. Through this agency, fresh eggs and milk, chicken, mutton or beef broth, bowl custard, and similar foods, are supplied. Medicines ordered by dispensary physicians or surgeons may be bought at the dispensary at a nominal uniform price of ten cents. In cases of extreme poverty, the physicians may order that the medicine be dispensed free of charge.

In connection with the dispensary, and under the care of the Harvard Medical School, is a station at which the services of a physician may be commanded night or day to attend women during childbirth at their own homes. These physicians are young men who are about to complete their medical education. They each have the assistance of a nurse. They are not only allowed but also expected to command the services of physicians skilled in midwifery whenever such services are necessary.

Other hospitals in Boston are of course equally open to the residents of this district; but those mentioned, being either in or so near it, are much sought by them. In this connection it is very gratifying to note the sentiment which prevails among the poor of the district in regard to going to a hospital. It is undoubtedly true that there is a constant lessening of the dread which is likely to exist in the minds of the poor, with regard to entering a hospital or seeking advice from its out-patient departments; and that such prejudices are being lessened is due to the almost uniform kindness and consideration, to say nothing of faithfulness, which are shown toward those who are treated at the hospitals, and toward their friends also. When a family has once had one of its

number at a hospital, that family is usually loud
in its praises of the care which the dear one received; and this is true, not only when the patient
recovers, but also in case of death. A similar atti-
tude is taken toward the dispensary. Both the
dispensary physician and the district nurse often
make themselves much beloved in the families
which they treat. That such a sentiment prevails
in regard to hospitals is most hopeful, showing as
it does that the work there accomplished does not
end with the mere setting of a bone or allaying of
a fever, but reaches far deeper, — even into the
real lives of the people.

There is one other class of institution in the
district which, although not established primarily
for that purpose, exerts an excellent influence over
the health of a certain portion of the tenement
dwellers; namely, the day nurseries. The direct
object of these nurseries is to furnish, during working hours, shelter, care, and food, for young children whose mothers are compelled to have employment away from home. Incidentally, however,
many of the minor ills which afflict childhood are
treated and relieved; and much instruction is
given the mothers regarding the proper care and
feeding of children.

It has been shown that the inhabitants of this

district live under certain conditions which tend to lower not only physical but mental and moral standards of health. These evil conditions are: the use of basements as dwelling-places, the overcrowding of buildings upon the land, insufficient street and park area, the overcrowding of tenements by their occupants, inadequate sanitary arrangements, and a lack of sufficient yard and clothes-drying space. Improvement in these matters must be brought about, through an illuminated public sentiment, by the enactment of new laws, of the City or the State, which shall more thoroughly safeguard the poor as to their homes. Certain other conditions which tend to lower the vitality of the people of the district are the result of ignorance and carelessness on their own part. Among these may be classed the keeping of windows shut against such ventilation as is accessible, the poor selection and bad preparation of food, and the abuse of alcoholic stimulants. For overcoming hostile influences of this kind we must rely upon the slow progress of education.

# CHAPTER V

## WORK AND WAGES

THE South End is as distinctly lacking in economic individuality as it is in any sort of local *esprit de corps*. One may frame a single conception of the North End, or of any of the outlying parts of the city in which working people live; but the South End is nondescript. To great numbers of Bostonians — such as know it at all — it is a kind of no-man's-land, through which, every day, they are whisked between their business headquarters in the heart of the city and their homes in Roxbury and Dorchester. A very large traffic rumbles through its streets without having any relation to it whatever, and a great part of the stream of people on its sidewalks have neither business duties nor home responsibilities within its borders. Moreover, one part of its resident population is of nomadic disposition; living in lodgings, they can be up and away without even the folding of tents. In a larger and slower but no less certain way, the present tenement-house population is shifting southward toward Roxbury little by little from year to year, forced on by the recent Continental influx.

Within the district specially under review, the chief industries are those associated with the coal slips and lumber yards on the water front, and with the factories which depend upon their supplies. The shipping interests of this part of the city are, however, considerably restricted by the fact that several drawbridges have to be passed before reaching the South Bay. Up and down along the docks lie a great proportion of the wood-working establishments of the city. Most of these are not large individually, but will be found congregated together in huge buildings, where the power is supplied from a common central source. A little farther from the water are the half-dozen piano factories, which represent the most interesting industry in the district. Partly in the same buildings with the wood-working factories, partly in independent structures specially adapted to their use, is an increasing number of steam laundries. The laundries find the central location of much importance in solving their problem of collection and delivery. The chief power-house plant of the Boston Elevated Railway, — formerly the West End Street Railway, — which controls all the electric cars in the city, is strategically placed, being

both at the centre of action and at the coaling base
of supply. The position of the district also locates
here several very large stables and many smaller
ones. There is the scattering variety of industrial
enterprise which might be expected; though it
must be remembered that Boston is not so great a
manufacturing city as its size would indicate. Following London from afar, it leaves manufacturing
to the smaller tributary cities and towns, and is
itself chiefly the emporium of trade and shipping.

None of the great department stores are in the
South End, though they undoubtedly attract the
great majority of local purchasers to their counters.
The most extensive commercial interests of this
vicinity are found in the installment stores, which
sell furniture or clothing on credit. Ground between these and the department stores, the small
shops which line all the main streets barely maintain themselves. By means of "cut prices" and
similar expedients they keep up a cheerful semblance of holding their own; but the night comes
when even the bravest may turn out its lights and
hang in the window a notice "Sold out to Ray-
mond," he being a disposer of the remains of dead
ventures. The proprietor then goes to work at
Jordan's or White's, and his clerk becomes perhaps
a street-car conductor. Of late even druggists

have been feeling keenly the rivalry of the patent-
medicine departments in some of the great downtown stores. The soda-water fountain, however,
is their hope and inspiration. Several large grocery and provision houses are located at the edge of
the commercial section; and there is a sufficiently
varied constituency to enable a rather high grade
of supply store to exist here and there through
the district. This kind of trade it is much more
difficult to focus in great central establishments.
The form of business which radiates most completely and clings most closely to the homes of the
people, so far as the South End is concerned, is
the liquor traffic. It represents the largest single
trade interest in the district; though it is to a
considerable extent capitalized from without, by
the system of "tied houses" held under the control of the great brewers. There is one substantial savings bank and one national bank; but the
characteristic local bankers are the pawnbrokers,
whose shop windows give a touch of tragedy to
Pleasant Street, the only winding, picturesque
thoroughfare at this end of the city. Commerce
comes to its simplest terms in the basement variety
stores found in the swarming back streets; in the
fruit stands and push carts of the Italians and
Greeks; in the omnipresent brazen-throated Irish

huckster with his horse and wagon; and in an improvised Jewish market, giving to the middle stretch of Harrison Avenue that odor of stale provisions which calls up poignant associations with the ghettos of Petticoat Lane and Hester Street.

It is the central situation of the district, rather than the industries actually carried on within its borders, that chiefly determines the occupation of its inhabitants. Even with this in mind, one would still be likely to overestimate the influence of the factories in giving character to the population. It is true here — as it is indeed in other large cities — that few skilled factory workers are found living near the scene of their work. When evening comes there is a rapid dispersion in every direction. There is besides no reason why skilled operatives engaged in other parts of the city should live in this part, — particularly when they have families. Men engaged in the building trades, who constantly shift their base of operations, may as well have their homes away from the crowd; and they are gradually realizing this. The proportion of the skilled in the district is kept up by the younger unattached mechanics and artisans living in the lodging houses, and often socially identified with the clerks. Of the men living in the best model tenement block, with one exception, to be

found in the district, there are thirty-eight artisans and sixty-one laborers. In a similar block,
owned by the same company half a mile beyond
the bounds of the district and on the edge of Roxbury, a good majority of the men represent skilled
trades. Even the sewing trades, which would
under ordinary conditions make such a locality
as this almost their own, have a disproportionately
small representation. This is because Massachusetts legislation against the sweating system has
practically abolished that iniquity in Boston; while
the general legislation of the State — including
the limitation of the weekly hours of work for
women and minors to fifty-eight, the prohibition
of child labor under the age of fourteen, and the
requirement of rather strict sanitary regulations —
prevents a low order of factory industry.

The characteristic industrial types of the district are those just above and just below the artisan,
— the clerk who easily walks to and from business
in the city, and wishes to be near its excitements
in the evening; the laborer who, from the lack
both of time and money, is compelled to make
his home close to the great activities of which his
toil is the foundation. A few of the clerks are
connected with well-to-do families still residing
in these parts. A larger number is made up of

those who belong to working-class families, and by reason of educational opportunities have risen in the economic scale, though still retaining their old family associations. The mass of the clerks, however, are young men from the rural parts of New England and from the British Provinces, who have their abode in lodging houses, and are making their first essay toward fortune behind the counter of a department store, or at the desk of some great corporation.

Laborers connected with the municipal departments constitute the aristocracy of the unskilled. " A job in the City " leaves nothing but " the force " as an object of ambition. The patronage controlling these labor appointments is distributed through the wards and allotted to the local politicians, subject to the form of a civil-service test.

Auxiliary to this is the labor staff of the great city monopolies, like the Boston Elevated Railway or the Boston Gas Company. Men are appointed to this in much the same way as to the City work, but it does not have the same atmosphere of dignity and ease about it. Failing either of these appointments, the ordinary laborer is attached to some builder or contractor. On a somewhat higher grade as to intelligence and skill is the large class of men employed in connection with

transportation interests. The four railroad stations along the downtown edge of the district —
now being united into a single great station —
furnish their representation of train hands, ex-
pressmen, and cabmen. The docks supply their
quota of water-side labor. Freight traffic, by rail
and by water, involves the employment of many
teamsters.

There is a large number of cooks, waiters, and
other employees of hotels and restaurants. These
are both men and women. Beginning on the
lowest scale of the distinctive work of women,
there is a considerable class of those who take
care of the cleaning in office buildings and stores,
or go out by the day for domestic work in the
neighboring residence sections. Every evening a
steady stream of factory girls comes out Harrison
Avenue, and as many shop girls return along the
superior social level of Washington Street. Most
of the work in the steam laundries is done by
women, who ordinarily live not far away from
their work. There is a scattering of skilled working-women in the dressmaking and millinery
trades. The number of women stenographers and
office assistants is small; they are found rather in
the superior grade of lodging houses west of Tremont Street.

In the way of dwellings, the district includes every sort, from the meanest rear tenement that can escape the authorities to the ample and imposing row with a park before it and a garden behind. One old family mansion remains, still inhabited by its original owners, bearing witness to the vanished glory of the South End. But it must not be thought that the mass of population has so wide a range of income as a person casually passing through its streets might suppose. By the decadence of the district, the newcomers were crowded even into the pleasantest neighborhoods. The houses thus taken possession of vary in grade according to the industrial standing of their new occupants, — but grade for grade they are in nearly all cases inconvenient and expensive, besides having the sanitary faults which have been pointed out in the previous chapter. There is, however, a refluent movement toward suitable conditions for families who must live in this congregate fashion. The numerous apartment houses, often misnamed "hotels," are usually suited to the means of well-to-do workingmen and small shopkeepers. For the rank and file of working people there are three groups of model tenements and an increasing number of newly built tenement houses designed to compete with the model buildings.

One must be cautious, however, about the sporadic yellow fronts which give gleams of brightness now and then through the Continental section of the district. These represent the Jewish passion for the unearned increment. At best they inclose the flimsiest of new structures. Often they are as whited sepulchres, — an old inner framework all untouched, the mud-colored bricks almost the only new or clean thing about them.

The floating population of the district is provided for by a considerable number of hotels, nearly all of which are evil resorts; and, on a lower scale, by a group of cheap lodging houses near the chief street crossing. The best of these lodging houses fall far short of the model establishments of the kind in New York and London. Under the more stringent rules lately put in force by the Board of Health two of them have, happily, been condemned.

In these cheap lodging houses — though some genuine workingmen are found there, and some men genuinely out of work — the tramp makes his winter quarters.[1] His daily income varies; but give him enough to pay for his night's lodging, with a friendly claim which insures his being "treated," and the world is all his own. From

[1] See Mr. Sanborn's *Moody's Lodging House*.

the roving pauper to the stationary is but a little
step.  One finds in the lowest tenement streets
an appreciable semi-pauperized class, — the evil of
pauperism being intrenched in drunkenness and
other degradation.  Taking the district as a whole,
there are many casual laborers who verge upon
this condition.  They frequently find work and
quickly lose it.  In the interim they are supported
by some relative, usually a woman.  They gain
occasional recuperation by several months at Deer
Island, but there is no lasting change.  No doubt
this class offers damaging irresponsible competition to steady, faithful workmen.  Certainly some
of them, by dint of political service, get City positions that ought to go at once to men capable and
worthy of them.

The problem of the unemployed has been during
the past five years an ever-present one.  No person who has lived here through these years could
question its actuality and seriousness.  Not many
months have passed during that time when there
have not been numerous respectable families of
working people that have been brought into severe
straits because their breadwinners for long periods
could find no work.  It is not the most efficient
workman, to be sure, who is thrown aside; but it
is by no means merely the moral delinquent that

suffers. The workman of moderate capacity, of
deficient education, of slight adaptability, or of
increasing years is ever the victim of apprehen-
sion. At times of severe business stringency, the
problem has assumed coherent form, and there
have been low, terrible murmurs half voicing the
most elemental of all human claims for justice.
Under ordinary circumstances, however, there are
not enough of the unemployed to classify themselves in that way. Those who are out of work
have their little savings, perhaps, or some other
member of the family comes to the rescue, or
they fall into the hands of charitable agencies;
but frequently they shift along in ways inconceiv-
able to every one but themselves. Even in its
milder, more dispersed aspect, the total burden of
this economic evil is a very heavy one, and it distinctly lowers the physical and moral tone of the
local community.

A little above the casual and unemployed
grades, there is a distinct element whose income,
while barely sufficient, is always intermittent, if
not positively insecure. This has been the case,
certainly of late years, with many artisans and the
unskilled labor dependent upon them. In every
form of garment work there is the regular rising
and falling according to season, varying in inten-

sity from year to year. In the piano factories, that first indication of financial depression which appears in the slackened demand for luxuries has many times of late put good workmen on the street. The colored men have a Rialto on Pleasant Street, at a point not far from several of the great hotels, into whose service they are drawn whenever there is exceptional need; but even if no man hire them, they do not seem to murmur or repine.

Lastly, there are the women who have to leave their homes to work by the day; very often they do not have as much employment as they need, but they represent no such problem as do the men in the occupations just mentioned.

Low regular wages brings a more satisfactory state of things than a high rate of wages with days in the week or months in the year when a man receives nothing. The poorest grade of unskilled labor, including some factory workers, is paid, when regularly employed, at the rate of nine dollars per week. It is fair to say that such men stand on about the same level as to labor and remuneration as the men in the East End of London who receive a pound a week; and here, as there, this type of man often sustains a happy, self-respecting home with this slight but secure

means of livelihood. Freight handlers, express-
men, and teamsters have this rate of wages as
their minimum, with perhaps twelve dollars per
week as their normal wage. Two dollars a day is
the fixed minimum rate for all City laborers; and
this standard more and more tends to regulate
similar labor, whether under quasi-public corporations or private contractors. For all outdoor
work this wage is not so large as it seems, because
there are many days lost during the year.

Many of the members of certain skilled trades,
such as bakers, waiters, and barbers, receive but
little, if any, higher wages than the mass of laborers; while garment workers, crushed by the competition of the most recent immigrants in Boston
and in New York, are as a rule happy to receive
the same weekly wage as the poorest of the unskilled. The best paid class of workmen is made
up of brick and stone masons, painters, plasterers, plumbers, machinists, structural iron-workers,
and other specially skilled artisans; cigar-makers,
conductors and motormen on the electric cars,
engineers, policemen, and firemen. The building
trades have larger wages than the rest, running
as high as $3.50 per day; but the other occupa-
tions more than make up for that by the security
of tenure the year round. Speaking generally for

this grade of work, wages run from $2.25 to $3.00 per day.

The superior grade of workmen having special skill, or charged with duties of superintendence, belong rather with clerks and tradesmen than with artisans; and they would rank high in such a class. Clerks are on about the same level as to income with artisans, considering that they are more regularly employed; but being generally without family responsibilities, they have more money to spend than the average of artisans. Small shopkeepers have a considerable range of income. On the whole, however, they are little if any better off, counting their long hours, than they would be as employees downtown; so that their problem reduces itself to that elemental human doubt, Is freedom worth responsibility?

The relative numerical strength of these different industrial groups can be ascertained with reasonable accuracy. For the casual and intermittent grades, the list of all those who receive some form of charitable relief each year may safely be taken. A calculation based upon the figures of the chief relieving agencies for the past seven years, completed from their estimates as to the amount of relief given by smaller charitable societies and by churches, shows that a little more than ten per

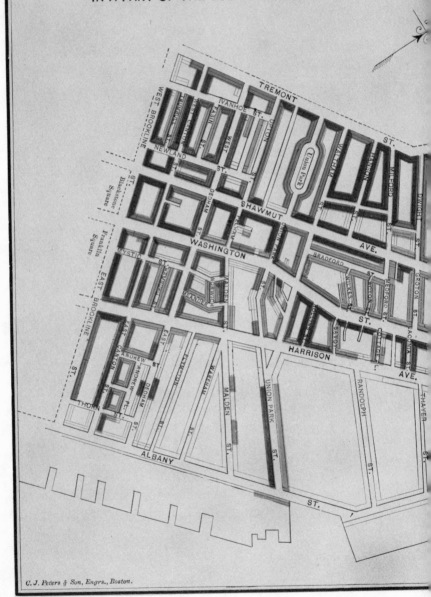

# MAP SHOWING THE
## INDUSTRIAL CHARACTER OF THE POPULATION
### IN A PART OF THE SOUTH END BOSTON

C. J. Peters & Son, Engrs., Boston.

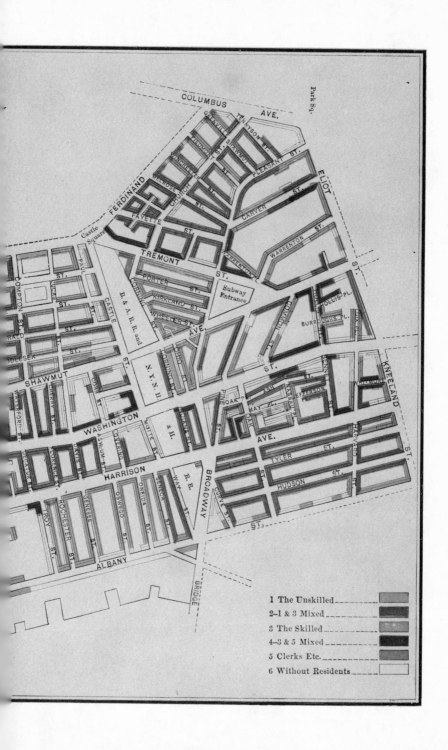

COLUMBUS AVE.

Park Sq.

GRANVILLE ST.
TENNYSON ST.
PIEDMONT ST.
SHAWMUT ST.
VINCENT ST.
PLEASANT ST.
MELROSE ST.
CHURCH ST.
FAYETTE
CARVER ST.
ELIOT ST.
FERDINAND
WARRENTON ST.
TREMONT
GREEN ST.
PORTER ST.
KIRKLAND ST.
Subway Entrance
WHEELER ST.
CORNING ST.
CASTLE ST.
B. & A. R. R. and
LOWNDE ST.
BURROUGHS PL.
HOLLIS PL.
Castle Square
COMPTON ST.
PAUL ST.
LUCAS ST.
N. Y. N. H.
OHIO ST.
WASHINGTON ST.
CORRY ST.
SHAWMUT
CHERRY ST.
& H.
PINE OAK
KNEELAND ST.
MAY ST.
OAK ST.
NASSAU ST.
JEFFERSON ST.
BENNET ST.
WILTON ST.
WATERFORD ST.
ALBION ST.
AVE.
WASHINGTON
MOTTE ST.
HARVARD ST.
TYLER ST.
HARRISON
DAVIS ST.
FLORENCE ST.
OVERING ST.
ASHLAND ST.
HUDSON ST.
UPSALL ST.
ONEIDA ST.
SENECA ST.
WAY R. R.
BROADWAY
CURVE ST.
ROCHESTER ST.
GENESEE ST.
OSWEGO ST.
ST.
ALBANY

BRIDGE

| | |
|---|---|
| 1 The Unskilled............ | |
| 2–1 & 3 Mixed............ | |
| 3 The Skilled............ | |
| 4–3 & 5 Mixed............ | |
| 5 Clerks Etc............ | |
| 6 Without Residents......... | |

cent of the population receive more or less of such help every year in the local district.[1]

Taking this as the proportion of the casual and intermittent classes, a small further allowance — certainly not more than one per cent — must be made for the professional loafer type. The floating population, as indicated by returns from the cheap lodging houses, would also make up one per cent, on the average.

With regard to the steady-going, industrious residents of the district, there are very satisfactory data. The City Board of Assessors compile in the spring of each year a complete list, by precincts and streets, of all the male inhabitants of the city who have passed their twentieth birthday, giving each person's occupation over against his name. The list for 1898 contains 13,815 names for this district. A classification and count of the occupations represented show that unskilled laborers, including a few inferior trades, number 5201 ; skilled workmen, receiving standard wages, 4411 ; clerks, superior workmen, and shopkeepers, 3577. Those entered as without occupation, chiefly old men, number 201. The remnant of professional men and downtown merchants foots up to 425.

[1] See the *Report of the Massachusetts Bureau of Statistics of Labor for 1892*, page 404 sq.

Some steps are necessary in order to secure percentages covering the entire population identified with these different economic levels. In the first place, there is a variation throughout the district of six per cent in the whole number of people which a given number of men represent, — more in the lodging houses, less in the tenement houses. The percentages thus gained must be altered by subtracting from them the twelve per cent credited to the loafer, casual, and intermittent classes; and we may safely charge a majority of these — seven per cent — to the unskilled laborers and a majority of the remainder to the skilled workmen. For the sake of simplicity, also, those without occupation may be distributed equally among the three chief classes. The result is, then: the unskilled labor class, regularly employed, twenty-eight per cent; the mechanic and artisan class, earning standard wages, thirty per cent; the clerk and shopkeeper class, twenty-seven per cent; the professional and mercantile class, three per cent.[1]

It is of course impossible to judge the economic standing of working-women from the wages they

[1] When these figures are compared with those of Mr. Charles Booth, it appears that upwards of seventy London districts, each containing three fourths as many people as the district here described, have in varying degrees a worse state of poverty than it

receive, because their responsibilities vary so much. One woman may work simply for money to spend on dress; another may have to provide for all her own wants, but nothing more; another still may be the breadwinner of a family. Women who go out to do cleaning by the day are paid at the rate of a dollar or a dollar and twenty-five cents. Factory girls receive as a rule five or six dollars a week. In case of rougher work, as in brush factories, the wages are even less. In steam laundries, on account of the element of danger, the average goes as high as eight or nine dollars; besides which the hours are shorter than the legal minimum. In the large stores, the low wages of the women — between four and five dollars a week on the average — are in a measure compensated by the eight-hour day, which was secured two years ago through efforts of the leaders of the Working-Women's Clubs.

The length of the working-day for wage-earners living in the district is reasonably satisfactory. To begin with, legal restrictions as to the hours of women and minors in factories practically also

has. Fully seventy-five per cent of the population of this district is above Mr. Booth's " line of poverty." The South End corresponds to parts of North London, and not to any of the typical poor districts of East or South London.

determine the hours of men working in association with them. Each organized trade has its own regulations. Carpenters work nine hours; masons, painters, and plasterers but eight. All City workmen come under the State requirement of the nine-hour day. Even the street-car men — a class most likely to be afflicted with long hours — are on duty during twelve hours, with but ten hours of actual work. The Saturday half holiday during the summer is now general in the large city establishments. A number of local grocery and provision stores, through the agency of the clerks' trade union, give a half holiday on Wednesday through the three warm months.

In the lodging and apartment houses of the district there is of course an appreciable number of salaried persons, — the higher grade of clerks in downtown offices, superintendents in stores and factories; and, among women, stenographers and bookkeepers. Only a few scattered individuals among the relics of a professional and mercantile class are men of any standing. Students, though numerous in other parts of the South End, are but few in number here. The really characteristic life of this inner half of the South End is, as has just been shown, not among the poor, not among the well-to-do; the district gets its distinctive qual-

ity from the struggling but sturdy working people.
Varying somewhat according to the number of
breadwinners in the family, and according to the
self-respect and thrift of the wife and mother, that
great class represents the local standard of income
and of expenditure.

It is always true throughout Boston that rent is
a very large item in the family budget ; but among
the working classes it makes a staggering burden.
Never less than one fourth, and often as much as
one third, of a workingman's income goes to the
landlord. In the territory under review, fully one
half of all the people live in what are commonly
understood as tenement houses. In at least 200
cases there is but one room to a family. The number of families living in two-room and three-room
tenements is upwards of 2500 ; the number of families living in four-room tenements is about 1800.[1]

Families living in one room pay from $1.25
to $1.75 per week for rent ; those living in two
rooms from $1.75 to $2.50 ; those living in three
rooms from $2 to $3 ; those living in four rooms
from $2.75 to $4. The one-room class represents
merely casual earnings ; the two-room class represents a family income of from $6 to $10 per week ;

---

[1] These estimates are based on the Tenement House Census of
1891–1892, made by the State Bureau of Statistics of Labor.

the three-room class, an income of from $7.50 to
$12 per week; the four-room class, an income of
from $12 to $15 and upwards per week. The two
and three room class constitute the majority of the
unskilled. Families having but two rooms often
use both rooms for sleeping purposes; those having
three rooms usually crowd the two tiny chambers
at night and reserve the larger room for all the
purposes of the day. If this room is kept clean it
is a presentable place for company; but the better
influences of home life and of social intercourse
begin with families having four rooms, one being
reserved for a parlor. To have a parlor gives a
family a strong and thoroughly commendable feeling of self-respect.

Rather less than one fifth of the population of
the district live in the highest grade of tenement
houses, apartment houses, and flats, paying a rental
of from $20 to $35 and upwards a month. Practically all of the remainder have their abode in
lodging houses, where furnished rooms are let at
from $1 to $5 a week, according to their size and
general desirability. Less than a hundred of the
families of the district have the happy lot to live in
houses by themselves, where the door leads immediately out to the open world, or shuts one in in-
stantly from its distractions.

The matter of the expenditure for food is quite largely a question of intelligence. Below the higher grades of labor the food selected is often ludicrously without nourishing value; it is badly cooked, and is eaten haphazard, with no regular time for meals. Brewed tea and the "growler" of beer play a very important part. Among the children the results of an insufficient supply of food are particularly noticeable. The common London practice of sending children to school without breakfast is not at all unknown in the South End. Homes in which the mother is a person of some resource naturally tell a better story; but even then there is a painful lack of all that art by which the housewife secures a variety of dishes at small cost, and turns all unused material to good account.

The cost of food, like that of rent, is very large in Boston. Even certain staples, like fish, for which Boston is the base of supply, are reported to cost more in Boston than in other cities farther inland. Not far from half of the income of working-class families in the district goes to this charge. The curse of the poor is their poverty. Families in the back streets are often kept by debt at the mercy of small dealers in dark corners and in basements; at best they can never afford the economy of buying in quantity.

The last few years have witnessed a very marked increase in the number of restaurants. This is true even in the Jewish quarter, where one would expect to find all the solitary set in families. The patrons of restaurants are not only single men and women, but married couples who live the dreary, demoralizing lodging-house existence because it seems to represent a social level which they could not maintain if they undertook housekeeping. There are two general types of restaurant. There are those along the business streets, offering meals *à la carte*. A few of these are of a high grade, but the large majority fully illustrate the abominations of the cheap restaurant. A number, good and bad as to food, are intended mainly for persons who come into the district upon questionable errands. Some of these restaurants are open, day and night, never having a key to the door. The other general type of restaurant is of a more domestic character. It is found in large numbers on the basement floor along the lodging-house streets. These restaurants exist because the conventional boarding-house is passing away. Their weekly terms are usually, " Gents, $3.50 ; Ladies, $3.00." Their larder and table companionship evidently do not grow rich with time, like old wine and old friends ; for they are always " under entirely new management."

The South End workingman counts out in advance fully three fourths of his income for rent and current household supplies. This leaves on his hands the problem of clothing his family and himself, furnishing his home, and reserving some slight margin for incidentals and savings. Too often the margin is so close that he attempts to gain ground by means of the installment store. This is quite generally done in purchasing furniture, and the business of selling clothing on the installment plan is apparently on the increase. It is only a step down from that to the pawnshop and " collateral loan " office. The thralldom under which many poor families are held by installment and loan establishments is most pitiable. It is not at all uncommon for them to have paid the full amount of a loan, including reasonable interest, and then to find there is just as much more still to be paid. Pawnshops are limited by law to a charge of from one to two and a half per cent per week, as the value of the pledges is higher or lower. A very satisfactory law has just been passed requiring all collateral loan offices — which differ from the pawnshops in not requiring mortgaged goods to be left on deposit — to be licensed by the Board of Police, as pawnshops are. The board is empowered to regulate the rate of interest to be charged, and to take instant action against all sorts of extortion. The rate has been fixed by the board at two per cent per month for amounts up to $50, and one and a half per cent for amounts between $50 and $200. It is hoped that this new plan will effectually prevent the brokers from taking advantage of the ignorance of their clients and of the secrecy with which such transactions are naturally surrounded.

The point at which resort is perhaps most often taken to the installment store is when there is good promise for the future and a family undertakes to have a parlor, with plush furniture and similar accessories. Families which have seen better days in the past are often found to be still struggling to pay installments, with the danger that their precious purchases will be taken from them, and the whole of what they have paid be lost. The installment system is regulated by law to the extent that where a purchaser has paid three fourths of his indebtedness the seller is permitted to take only so much of the value of the goods as will meet the rest of the bill. This prevents confiscation on the dealer's part, but it seldom saves loss on the debtor's part. The prices placed on installment goods are notoriously high, and they are forced on poor people in all sorts of plausible ways. The system roots itself, however, in certain weaknesses of human nature, and is hardly capable of being further restricted.

Taking the people of the district grade by grade, dress would often but slightly suggest home conditions. Food and shelter are taxed to support the clothing fund. Among the young men and women, the young women especially, it is surprising to find what becomingly dressed persons can come out of really miserable abodes. Many of the young women, working in dry-goods stores, dressmaking and millinery establishments, make their patrons serve as their models. It is gratifying that in their endeavor they follow many of the restraints which their exemplars illustrate. There is comparatively little vulgar finery to be seen on the thoroughfares, even among the class of women who are supposed to parade that. In tenement streets, the shawl still does general utility duty among older women, — a function which the gossamer waterproof, rain or shine, concealing tawdriness more completely but more obviously, seems to fill with the younger generation. Adorned or unadorned, many of the people of the tenement houses, badly housed, badly fed, are also, so far as protection is concerned, badly clad. Certainly in winter a considerable proportion of the children go about with garments wholly insufficient against the east wind. One is glad to say that there rarely appear here any of those ragged, battered types, with hardly the human semblance left, such as the popular imagination associates with congested poverty.

In the aggregate a very considerable expenditure is to be charged to religion and recreation. Few, if any, of the Protestant churches can depend entirely upon local support, but the Roman Catholic churches are sustained by their immediate adherents with a loyalty that is hardly less astonishing for not being altogether spontaneous.

The chief outlay for amusements goes to the theatre. A part of the regular fees paid for membership in clubs and lodges also comes under this head. Among the higher grades of working people an appreciable amount of the year's income goes for excursions and vacation trips; but where a man's income is below the working-class average, even a day's outing in the parks or at the beaches is — for his whole family — almost too expensive an undertaking.

Thrift has the final residuary claim. This virtue would have more devotees if the ascent to it were not so steep. When the head of the family is a victim to drink, it is impossible. Indeed, drink tends to blot out all the economic relations touched on in this chapter. It first impairs and then lays aside the producer. Under its power the purchaser of commodities first gives up thrift; then the amenities of life disappear ; then there is no new clothing, and all that is fit to wear goes to the pawnshop ; presently the family has to borrow or beg its food; at last there is an eviction. Aside from extreme individual results, the well-nigh universal custom of " taking a little " means an appalling wasteful drain on the resources of the local population.

Between families tending upwards and those tending downwards, thrift, being the first thing undermined, may be taken as a sure distinguishing mark. In certain forms thrift is very general, such as child insurance. This is, however, only improvidence in disguise ; the insurance money always goes for an expensive funeral. A higher and less common condition is that of having a savings bank account. Membership in trade unions, benefit societies, lodges, and coöperative banks illustrates still more advanced foresight. Families that rise into comparatively easy circumstances do so by living for a long time in meaner quarters than their incomes would well provide, or by taking lodgers, or by the mother's energy in

the way of securing work outside of her domestic
duties. Sometimes families gradually purchase
the houses in which they live. In many cases
local property is still owned by working-class residents of years ago.

It is worth while to note certain influences which
affect the general economic standards of the people in such a district as this. Some of these influences, increasing the range and raising the level
of desire and taste, come out of the essential conditions of American life. This country insists upon
assimilating all new-comers; that is, not merely
teaching them its political traditions, but imparting to them its ampler way of existence. Such
great common institutions as the public school, the
press, and the right of free discussion, — the public school especially, — show their elevating power,
amongst the population of the South End, not only
in the spread of knowledge but in the distinct
industrial rise, individual and collective, of the
second generation of the different foreign nationalities. The American people are a selection of
enterprising spirits, and we presuppose, even in
the most recent immigrant, a degree of personal
ambition. Opportunity is not so ever present, and
success is by no means so rapid or so general as it
once was; but the fact that in every group of ac-

quaintances in the district some one is prosperous
is a constant stimulus to greater effort on the part
of all. Even in the face of the most untoward
circumstances — and without making light of the
crushing power of the circumstances that surround
the life of poverty — one can often find here
some touch of that dauntlessness which is typi-
cally American.

The peculiar relation of the district to the rest
of the city, the coming and going of all classes of
people, keep it from falling into that extreme
slackness which is characteristic of most working-
class quarters in great cities. The great thoroughfares, as the public meeting-place and exchange,
have the effect of keeping up the economic tone
of the district; one would hardly imagine, from
a walk out Washington Street, that there was
a large amount of actual poverty on both sides.
The theatres, and to a smaller extent the churches,
serve this same purpose, by bringing together, not
only different sorts of South End people, but
people as well from the other parts of the city and
from the suburbs.

Though the lack of friendly association between
the Back Bay and the South End is so complete
that there is no direct street-car communication,
yet it must not be said that the two sections have

no dealings with each other. The Back Bay, which sometimes "investigates" the South End, would probably be surprised to know how constantly it is being in turn investigated by means of back-door and below-stairs points of approach. The leader of the "smart set" is a story-book heroine here; and if South End folk cannot be at the wedding feast of the great heiress, some of them can at least stand outside — rain will not dampen their ardor — and cheer her as she enters her equipage. Besides this dream-stuff, however, the district has its own solid social ambitions, which, unlike the shallow and often cruel pretensions of the upper circles, go with distinct personal achievement. It is not altogether an evil that the policeman's wife considers herself " away up in society," with a sort of official reputation to sustain, and that she stands as an object of emulation to those not breathing that serener air.

Judging from appearances, it might seem an advantage to the people of the South End that it is so closely bound to the city's chief business centre and its chief centre of social power. There is the semblance of gain in the loss of local economic independence. Such a view is forbidden, however, by two great facts specially involved in the situation of this district: family and neighbor-

hood life compressed together, and made thick and
sluggish by the cohesive energy of the surrounding
city; people with vitality and vigor thus lowered
met by the evil contagion that comes with the floating crowd.    The fundamental economic wrongs
which affect working-class life everywhere find
strong intrenchment in such a situation.

# CHAPTER VI

## THE ROOTS OF POLITICAL POWER

IT is not the purpose of this chapter to discuss methods of political reform, but to show the play of personal and social forces beneath the surface of boss rule and ward politics. To do this, it is necessary at the very beginning to understand the prevalence and power of gangs, and their methods of organization. The importance of the gang as a social factor which the politician manipulates has never been fully appreciated except by the politician. It is a sufficiently commonplace trait of human nature for people to associate themselves together in groups and cliques, according to the attractions of congeniality. This force, however, seems to work with great intensity in the tenement-house districts. Without pausing to inquire the reasons, I shall describe the structure of the gang, and later show its relation to ward politics.

The tendency begins among the children. Almost every boy in the tenement-house quarters of the district is member of a gang. The boy who does not belong to one is not only the exception, but the very rare exception. There are certain characteristics in the make-up and life of all gangs. To begin with, every gang has a " corner " where its members meet. This " hang out," as it is sometimes called, may be in the centre of a block, but still the gang speak of it as the " corner." The size of a gang varies : it may number five or forty. As a rule, all the boys composing it come from the immediate vicinity of the corner. Every gang has one or more leaders; and of course its character depends very much upon the leaders, for as one of the boys exp essed it the leader says " ' Come,' and the push move." As a matter of fact, a gang if at all large has two leaders and sometimes three. In order to show the different kinds of leadership, let me describe the qualities possessed by the three types in a large gang. First of all, there is the gang's " bully." He is the best " scrapper " in the gang. Many a hard - won battle has paved the way to this enviable position ; but the position, often attained with so much difficulty, is not a sinecure. The bully not only has to defend the honor of the gang, but may have to defend his title at any time against the ambition of some " growing" member of the gang. Next there is the gang's "judge;" all matters in dispute are finally submitted to him if no agreement is reached. The boy who enjoys this honor has gained it not by election but by selection. The boys have gradually found out that he does not take sides, but is fair minded. Finally there is the gang's "counselor," — the boy whom the gang looks to for its schemes both of pleasure and of mischief. In small gangs the bully may also be the judge and counselor, and even in large gangs it frequently happens that one boy dispenses both the latter functions. Here is the ward boss in embryo.

Nightly after supper the boys drift to their "corner," not by appointment, but naturally. Then ensue idle talk, "jawing matches," as one boy expressed it, rough jokes, and horse-play. No eccentric individual gets by the gang without insult. Nearly every gang has "talent": one or two members who can sing, perhaps a quartette; also a buck-dancer, one or two who can play on the jew's-harp, and a "funny man." I am referring now more particularly to boys over fourteen years old. As a rule, the boys stay around their corner, finding amusement in these ways. The songs are always new ones; old ones are scorned. Not infrequently the singing, the horse-play, or

the dancing is interrupted by the roundsman.
At the sight of the brass buttons, there is an
excited call of "cheese it," and singing or talking,
as it may be, is suddenly stopped; the gang dis-
bands, dissolves, and the boys flee down alleyways,
into doorsteps and curious hiding-places, and
reappear only when the "cop" is well down the
street.

It sometimes happens that members of the gang
are arrested, for standing on the corners, for in-
sulting passers-by, or for some other offense. As
a rule, the other fellows raise the money to pay
the fine. To reimburse themselves or the one
who loaned the money, a dance is "run" or a
raffle is held. To show still further the tenacious-
ness of gang life: the influx of Jews has caused
many of the Irish to move away from the South
End to other parts of the city, but the boys on Sunday may be found with the gang at their corner.
About thirty young men belonging to one of the
gangs I know, meet every Sunday afternoon at
their corner. Of this number, fully half are fellows who live in the Highlands, at the edge of
Roxbury. I know a boy in the High School — he
will graduate next year — who moved to Dorchester, but comes regularly to the old corner on Sunday afternoon. No new friends can supplant the

gang. It is little wonder. The life of the gang is exciting, melodramatic; the corner is full of associations, of jokes and songs and good times, of escapades planned and carried out. In comparison with this, the life of the suburb is tame.

It is interesting to know what becomes of these various gangs when the boys get to be seventeen or eighteen years old. The more respectable gangs, as a rule, club together and hire a room. The more vicious gangs prefer to use what little money they have in carousing. If by any chance they get a room, their rowdyism will cause their ejection either by the landlord or by the police. Consequently they have to fall back on the corner or some saloon, as their meeting-place. They nearly always seek a back street or the wharves, unfrequented by the police.

Not infrequently these gang connections are tenacious in the case of older men, who sometimes meet in the back of some store to play " forty-five," but more often would be found in a favorite saloon. In numerous cases a saloon serves as a club room for one or more gangs of these older men, who are loyally devoted to it. Many of them will walk by saloon after saloon thirsty, in order to reach a particular drinking place with enough money to secure the proprietor's welcome.

At this point, it is necessary to give some account of the young men's clubs, in order that the important part that these clubs play in ward politics may be seen; for all this network of social life is taken in hand by the politician. As I said before, the gangs which coalesce and form these clubs are the most respectable ones. They are led to do this partly through a desire to have a warm room, and partly because they are tired of standing on the corner and meeting the rebuffs of the policeman. Then such a club opens up the freedom of the district, socially, to them. The first month or two is a trying time for every new club. Each gang composing it is likely to have a candidate for the principal offices; and frequently the first election is the occasion for a quarrel between the rival gangs, which breaks up the club before it is well begun. There are about eight of these clubs in the particular section which I know best. The dues range from twenty-five to fifty cents per week, and the club pays usually from $25 to $35 per month for its room.

Nearly all of the clubs have a common programme. In the first place, each club, without any exception, gives a ball each winter in some large hall. The tickets invariably sell for fifty cents. These balls are important social functions in the district. As a rule, they are well managed financially, one club clearing $165 last winter. Then besides this annual ball, each club has a " social" once a week. This is a dance of a lower type than the balls, being interspersed with comic songs, humorous recitations, and buck dancing. About the same class of girls attend all the socials; they go from one club to the other. Almost without exception they are factory girls, and nearly all of them are bold and vulgar. It is a curious fact that the members do not want their sisters to attend these dances; and their custom is to leave the girls with whom they have danced before they reach the street. If you should enter the room of one of these clubs on the night of a social, about ten o'clock, you would have to push your way through a crowd of fellows blocking the entrance and massed against one side of the room, nearly all smoking, with hats on, and making " cracks " and " breaks," as they express it, at every newcomer.

Another feature of these clubs is the smoke talks. They are always held on holidays, and sometimes on Sundays. Several barrels of beer are on tap; and tonic is ordered for abstainers, but they are few. The smoke talk usually begins in the afternoon, and lasts as long as the beer

does. When the end comes, those who are sober
are in the minority. For entertainment there
are comic songs and buck dances, but the principal feature is the story-telling. There are some
fellows who tell such a good story that they get a
considerable local reputation and are much sought
after for these occasions. The singers, dancers,
and story-tellers are in fact so many strolling
merrymakers, and are welcome at all the clubs.
Fancy a room dim with smoke, men freely drinking, some arguing, some maudlin drunk, some
cross and pugilistic, others funny, a half-tipsy
story-teller reeling off a yarn in one part of the
room, and presently the noise of a brass band
or the click - click of the buck dancer, and you
will get some idea of that queer thing, a smoke
talk.

Each club has its unemployed, who live no one
knows exactly how. Some clean up the room and
thus save their membership. The fellows who
work supply them — in part out of good-nature
and club feeling — with drinks and tobacco. The
room is open in the daytime, and here those out
of work can come and play cards and loaf. This
contingent is known as the " day club." Very frequently they are the companions of girls who work
in factories; and receive weekly subsidies out of the

girls' earnings. In some cases they impose upon
their mothers or sisters who work, and thus secure
their board at home, and perhaps a little pocket
money.

The worst dance halls are very nearly allied to
the clubs, for all the halls have their special clientage. This clientage, like the club, is made up,
though not so distinctly, of gangs. Consequently
at nearly all the halls, the dancers are known to
one another, and have more or less loyalty for the
hall. At one hall a large group of fellows attend,
nearly all of whom have stylish light coats and
dudish attire, even if they do not know where the
next meal is coming from. In winter their mis-
tresses support them. In summer these men are
fakirs and go to Nantasket and the beaches, and
in the fall they take their gambling outfits to fairs
at Brockton and elsewhere.

The description thus far of the gang, the social
club, and the dance hall, shows that the politician
does not need to deal with individuals. Ready at
hand are these various social centres for him to
make use of.

In addition to these social groups which take on
a political character at election time, there are
usually in the tenement-house sections several distinctly political clubs. Standing at the head of

these clubs is the "machine club." It is now quite the custom of those in control of the party, and known as the "machine," to have such an organization. All the men in the ward having good political jobs are members. In one local club it is estimated that the City employees belonging to it draw salaries to the amount of $30,000 per year; in another club, outside the district, $80,000. It is natural that all the men in these clubs are anxious to maintain the machine. It is a question of bread and butter with them. In addition to City employees the various machine workers are enrolled. The room of the club is ordinarily very pleasant. There are, of course, in these clubs the usual social attractions, among other things poker and drinking. At the head of the club stands the boss of the ward.

So much for the organizations which are manipulated for political ends. The various typical actors in ward politics must now be described; first, the boss, his lieutenants, and "heelers." One of the bosses whom the writer knows is fairly typical. He is considered the "prince of jolliers," on account of his alluring ways. He has for many years been in public office of one kind or another. His early opportunities were small. His native abilities, however, enable him to fulfill his official duties with real effectiveness, — when political business does not interfere. As he not infrequently plays the rôle of Warwick in politics, he gets a glimpse of larger worlds to conquer. These, however, can exist for him only as tantalizing dreams, for the lack of that education possessed by many whom he brushes aside and scorns. He does not reap the rich harvest which comes to the members of his craft in other cities. He does not carry with him any of the obvious signs of marked prosperity. He would probably not refuse greater spoils, however. The possibilities in that direction in Boston are limited mainly to deals in connection with contracts for City works and supplies. The great corporations can only be nettled; they cannot be leeched. Their larger privileges are decided upon by the legislature. Even the licensing and police powers are retained by the State. It is to some extent the love of authority that urges the boss on. He knows his power, his mastery over men. There is one quality which this typical boss has that gives him a sort of moral leadership. He makes many general promises which he never intends to fulfill, but a specific promise he usually keeps. He is distinguished among the politicians of the city as being a man of his word. This is

honesty or sagacity, as you choose to look upon it.
There must be a certain degree of honor in dividing the spoils of politics, and the politician must
provide something with which to feed his hungry
followers. The jobs that he tries to get for his
followers, however, are not secured as the private
employer seeks men, — for efficiency. The motive
of the boss in seeking favors from the City government is to satisfy claims against him and to maintain himself. In this, forsooth, he considers himself as merely going the way of the world. He
is to a large extent justified in so thinking. The
highly respectable contractor or corporation man,
for instance, who directly or indirectly makes corrupt deals with him, does so because "business is
business." The boss enters into these deals, and
goes through the rest of his programme, not because he likes to, but because "it's politics." Both
are caught in the toils of an evil system.

The boss has reduced to a science the knack
of dominating men. If a "jolly" or the "glad
hand" will not carry his point, he can quickly
frown. The frown of the boss is supposed to
carry terror to the hearts of those to whom he
has rendered favors, or who expect jobs. This
is easily accounted for, as without his approval
no one in the ward can get a City job.

On the whole, partly for the love of position and power, and partly from a good heart, the boss enjoys doing good turns for men. Stories are told by his admirers of his generous deeds. For instance, he has been known to pay the funeral expenses of poor people who have no insurance. At Christmas time and Thanksgiving he gives turkeys to certain needy families. Dance tickets, baseball passes, tickets to the theatre, railway passes, and so forth, — which cost him nothing, being simply incidental results of his tools in the common council or the legislature voting " right," — are distributed with wise discrimination. He is always ready to treat. Some go so far as to say that if he died to-morrow his friends would have to pay his funeral expenses. This all sounds very generous ; but the chief admirers of the boss cannot deny that when the supremacy in the ward is at all endangered, he makes capital of all his good deeds. In other words, every man to whom he has granted a favor is made to feel that the boss expects a vote.

I do not see how any man in his position, however good his character to begin with, could do otherwise than use men as checkers on a board. His ambition to boss the party in his ward necessitates his looking upon men continually from the

point of view of votes. The logic of the boss
system demands this. Votes are his business, —
they mean money, power. The boss can never be
a disinterested member of society. He is forced
to make men act and vote with him, — the weaker
their wills, the fewer their convictions, the better
for him. He gives another drink to the drunkard : he has a vote. The only morality he seeks
in men is loyalty to him. The merit system he
regards always with a horror and indignation which
would be amusing if it were not so serious.

I said the boss knew how to domineer. For
instance, two years ago his rule met with considerable opposition. A group of men got together,
put up a fairly strong ward and city committee,
and selected one of their number to run for warden,
as a guarantee of an honest caucus. The boss
grew suddenly active. He quickly visited about
half the men on the ticket. Some he warned that
if they ever wished a City job, he would oppose
them ; others he smiled upon, promising them election to an office later on, or a position in a City
department if they would only withdraw. He
came to the room of their leader, having learned
that he had some intention of running for a certain
office later on. Almost before greeting this man,
the boss demanded that he withdraw his name as

warden from the opposition ticket.  Bringing his
fist down on the table, and growing purple in the
face, he swore with a horrible oath, that if this
man did not withdraw his name, he could never
be elected to any office in the ward.

The boss is always strictly orthodox in his politics; he is intensely partisan.  Independency is the
unpardonable sin in his eyes.  He grows really
eloquent over "party harmony;" he storms and
raves, he plots, he pleads, for party harmony.  He
is really in earnest.  His constituency like this
loyalty of his, too.  He deceives them.  Sometimes
he deceives himself.  He always knows, however,
that party harmony brings greater party success,
more patronage, larger favors from corporations.
Party harmony does not mean to the boss the
greater ascendency of party principles; it stands
to him for good business, greater returns.

I will speak here of one more characteristic of
the boss, reverting to some of his ways later on
in describing the caucus.  Political gossip is intensely interesting to a great many people.  The
boss makes the most of this interest.  He knows
how to keep a secret and he also has the art of
telling as a secret what he wants published on the
housetops.  There is something very flattering in
having the boss retail to you the political gossip

of " downtown." He does this the most effectively at the club, or at a saloon, where a crowd
quickly gathers.  In this rôle he is quite at his
best when he speaks in scathing terms of some
opponent, or perhaps the " fight " at a recent con-
vention.  It is racy, pugilistic talk.  It is cheap,
but it keeps the boss in touch with the crowd.
If washed down with a drink, it makes the boss
a good fellow, " one of our kind," the idol of
the tough element, — and the tough element tell
mightily in a caucus.

There are certain lesser figures characteristic of
ward politics known as " heelers."  They do the
dirty work.  As a rule, they prefer to serve the
well-established boss, as he can best protect them
if they are found out and prosecuted in the execution of their villainy.  As a rule, a " heeler " is a
broken-down " bum," afraid of work, fond of his
cups, in touch with loafers and the semi-criminal
class, more of a fox than they, energetic enough
in a campaign, possessed of a strong dramatic
sense, loving the excitement of ward politics with
its dark plots and wire pulling, glad to be lifted
into temporary importance by having money to
spend on the " boys."

Some personal touches may make the heeler a
little more real.  One whom I know wears eye-

glasses, which are in picturesque contrast to the unshaven face, filthy white shirt partly hidden by a frayed necktie, and more filthy clothes sadly in need of repair. Once, on the eve of election,—when therefore he had some money in his pocket,—I remember he had on a clean collar and a new tie, but the shirt was still dirty. Perhaps his ambition stopped short of a clean shirt—it meant just so much drink. He lives with a " policy writer " and occasionally helps him in his work. In reality a bar-room loafer, he knows the semi-criminal class and " bums " better than any one else in the ward. He is just as fond of loafing as the idlest one of the lot. Consequently he is known to them as " their kind," but his intelligence and " gift of the gab " make him a leader. He has a " frog in the throat " voice, which becomes barely a croak by caucus night. His method of buttonholing and poking out his head at a man, in very earnestness, is well calculated to be convincing. He really has considerable managing ability; and if he were clean for once and had a new suit, you might easily place him as a factory manager or a captain in a regiment.

Another heeler I know of moved into the ward some time ago from a tough neighborhood. He was the best fighting cock on the street. He is only a little fellow, but can stand no end of "punishment." Whether his reputation rests as much on the number of blows he can give as on the number he can receive, I do not know. In addition to his pugilistic reputation, he is known as a "pool shark." He plays very successfully a game known as "one ball," which is very popular in many billiard rooms on Saturday nights. In addition to making money by this method of gambling, he is another example of that rather numerous class of unspeakably diseased and dissipated men who keep company with and share the money of certain prostitutes, too frequently browbeating them, and occasionally scouting for their victims. In the gambling fraternity, of which he is a shining light, he has of course a following which he can command.

Another heeler who is fairly typical comes of a rather respectable family and lives at home. He is a hard drinker and noted fighter; he occasionally gets arrested. Once in a while he secures a City job and does a little work. He knows how to throw down a half dollar in this or that saloon in the most approved fashion, and call for a general toast to the success of some "regular" candidate. For four or five years he has been a caucus checker. In a tight election he is noted for his ability in deftly copying from the check list, late in the evening, names of those who have not voted, — so that they may be used by "repeaters." He is also like many other heelers in standing on the corners and about saloons and, according to the expressive language of the district, "chewing the rag," — which signifies arguing.

Repeaters are important actors in ward politics. It is a curious fact that there are many men belonging to the loafing and semi-criminal class who, because of their nerve, can repeat at a caucus so deftly that they are regarded as "expert repeaters." They are known to the boss or his heelers, and are often employed in close elections. They of course feel fairly secure under the protection of the boss. One fellow whom I know boasted to me that in a certain election he was driven from ward to ward, changing his disguise occasionally, and voting eight times in the course of the day. On inquiry, I found it was in all probability true. Another man has a City job, but seldom works. He is a "valuable repeater," useful to the boss; the City pays, and the boss is strong enough to make his tenure secure. There are fellows who, without thought of doing wrong, repeat once in a while for some friend up for office. They are accounted respectable young men in the community.

They say, "The others do it; we've got to do it to win."

Besides the boss, his lieutenants, and his heelers, there are usually in all tenement-house wards a large number of aspirants for some elective office; together with the incumbents of such positions and some retired politicians. They all have their clientage. Occasionally one will find a man who is honest, and really wants to see an honest caucus, honest legislators, and civil service reform. Such men are few in number, however; and while a candidate of that kind will always be lauded in the campaign circulars by his followers for his honesty, his best friends will secretly wonder and shake their heads at his eccentricity. It is impossible to convince the knowing ones that any candidate is not "out for the stuff."

Men with a trade, or small contractors, will tell their friends openly that they want office because it will help them in their business. Apparently no thought enters their minds that they are seeking office for wrong ends. Furthermore, such an argument is forceful with numbers of the rank and file of voters. The painter expects a City contract; the young man desiring a liquor license not infrequently seeks to go to the common council for a "character recommendation," in order that he may the more readily secure a license. The point of view of the majority of candidates and voters, too, is that the municipal government is theirs to use. Of course, all these men have their following. Some are friendly to the boss, others not.

In analyzing ward politics, it is necessary to understand something of the morale of the various groups of voters. As to race complexion, in the local wards the Irish voters prevail. Next in number are the Jews. There is a good sprinkling of " Yankees," a term which for political purposes includes the British element. Foreigners other than those mentioned do not cut much of a figure in politics. It goes without saying that the greatest degree of political activity is found among the Irish. The Jews, however, are commencing to take considerable interest in politics. The most earnest and unselfish of them are Socialists, but some of them are quite as keenly after the main chance as the Irish politician. In one of the wards of the district [1] there are five hundred Jewish voters. In justice to them it must be said that it is as yet early to prophesy what their position in politics will be. The social rela-

[1] The district includes Ward 7 (except one precinct), Ward 9, two precincts of Ward 10, and parts of two precincts of Ward 12.

tions of the Irish and the Jews are not very cor-
dial. There seems to be a special antipathy ordinarily on the part of the Irish for the Jews. Not
so with the Irish politician. He solves the race
problem in short order. He fraternizes with the
Jew, eats with the Jew, drinks with the Jew, and
dickers with him in politics.

I have spoken of the large number of young
men enrolled in social clubs, and in describing the
activities of the clubs have suggested the character
of their members. In these wards there is a large
number of men in the employ of the City, chiefly
as laborers. I have already referred to the loafers and semi-criminal class. Many of them live
in lodging houses. It is a tradition among these
men to stand in with the boss. If they get into
trouble with the police, he frequently comes to
their assistance. Through his help, the case is
sometimes quashed or the sentence is abridged.
This is the rough contingent that always attends
the caucus and drives many respectable citizens
away.

In noting the various classes of voters in these
wards, it is also necessary to keep steadily in mind
the large number of unemployed men. In the
study of ward politics this factor has not been
sufficiently appreciated. I do not refer now to the

loafers, but to the honest unemployed. The number of men who are almost ready to fawn upon one
for a job is simply appalling. Ask those in the
settlements, at the charity headquarters, the mission churches, or the workingmen's resorts, and
they will tell you the same story. Some of these
men are looking for political jobs. Consider the
hold the boss can gain upon them. The few secure
a job; the many get promises. Those who get
jobs are the slaves of the boss. He does not make
the work, and there is no credit in what he does,
but you cannot blame them for their slavery.
What is the honest use of their suffrage compared
with bread? According to the ethics of the district, a man who receives a job is under the most
sacred obligations to the politician who bestowed
it. The lack of employment, therefore, is one of
the most important factors working in the interest
of the boss and boss rule.

There is still another group that must be mentioned. There is in these wards a considerable
number of young men who regard politics as El
Dorado. They are poor but ambitious. Many
of them have received a fairly good education. It
more and more requires a " friendly pull " in order
to secure a good position in business. In business, too, they have to meet strong prejudices

of race and religion. Politics, therefore, is for
them apparently the easiest way to success in life.
In every ward such as we are describing, there are
a few conspicuous examples of men living in comfort, who are reported rich, and have made their
money in politics. It is told you, for instance,
that the mother of one of these men lived in a
garret and went barefoot out of sheer poverty.
Thus the clever young fellow is encouraged to try
his hand. Politics means business. Moral scru-
ples are brushed aside. Victory at the caucus is
the gateway of fortune.

The saloon in its relation to politics has already been referred to somewhat, and one need
only touch upon it here in order to give it the
proper place in this picture of ward politics. In
each ward of such a section as this, it is safe to
say that there are five or six hundred men who are
more or less influenced by the political talk of the
saloon. As has already been shown, gangs often
use particular saloons as club-rooms. The men
who frequent the saloons are, almost without exception, the men who attend the caucus. They are
naturally influenced a great deal by the saloon-
keeper, whom they see almost daily. Drinking
makes men sociable ; and if a barkeeper is given
money with which to treat the boys, even the

fairly respectable men who are at the bar, after a round of drinks, look with favor upon the saloon keeper's candidate. The saloon is thus the place where political opinion is formed very quickly, and the opinions formed there are soon circulated through the community by the " saloon gossips." No man who wishes to become elected in these wards disregards the saloon. Other things being at all equal, the man who has the greater number of saloon keepers on his side will surely be elected.

The method of assessing and registering men is one of the most effective means of securing a considerable vote. This is attended to mainly by the ward heelers. Much of the work of having men assessed and registered before election time is legitimate ; much is perjury. For instance, in a close election, if the candidate cares to spend the money, he can commission these heelers to draw in acquaintances of theirs, men from other wards or men without a fixed address, who for a slight consideration are willing to be assessed and registered. The law provides that a man can vote only in the ward where he lived on the first of May previous to the election. Some address is given the man, and he and the heeler swear that he lived there on the first of May. A certificate is

given, and by virtue of the certificate the bearer is
allowed to vote. If the warden of the caucus does
not stamp the certificates, they can be used over
again. The men guilty of these corrupt practices
could be detected and prosecuted, but they are
not. For lack of witnesses it would be very hard
to make out a case. The ethics of the district
would brand evidence giving as " squealing," and
the life of a witness would be made unendurable
thereafter.

In nearly all tenement-house wards, one party
is strongly in the majority.[1] Such being the
case, a nomination at the caucus usually means
an election at the polls. The caucus is therefore
the place where the real contest occurs. There is
no single event in the ward that can equal the
caucus for interest. It is a scene where the various
gangs meet, as so many tribes, and fight for supremacy; where ambitious young men strive together
for a " start " in life; where fortunes are made
and lost; where sensational attempts are made to

---

[1] The minority party of this district is left out of account because of its local insignificance, not because of its freedom from
corruption. In City elections it has money to spend. At such
times useful heelers and leaders of gangs, belonging to the majority party, often depart for a few weeks from their regular
allegiance.

"down" the boss; it is a scene where a strong, rough, "jollying" personality tells as in the good old days of the fighting barons. Again, it is a busy mart where men are bought and sold, a place where the drunkard can get the price of another drink, a place full of surprises, of unsuspected combinations, of damaging circulars sprung too late for answer, of small leaders fighting under new banners. It is besides the great social event for the men of the ward, when they gather in crowds and push and jostle and "jolly" and joke, and yell for their favorite, and bet on him as they might bet on horses. It is, moreover, a leveling event; an event in which the "thug" feels, not as good, but better than his more respectable neighbor. Finally the caucus is a place of action. It is the great ward drama — full of strong human touches, too often potent in tragedy to free institutions and the common welfare.

In case a boss is likely to be strongly opposed at a caucus for the election of ward officers, he can afford to spend a large sum of money in his campaign. How much he can afford to spend is in the main simply a question of business — of addition and subtraction. He stands, aside from the ambition to rule men, to get as much as possible out of politics for himself and the "gang."

It is not necessary, usually, to spend much money direct for votes. Beer in the saloons, "beer parties" at the social clubs, and "house parties," getting work for the leaders of doubtful gangs, bailing a member of a tough gang out, employment of heelers to assess and register men falsely, and "circulars," are some of the common methods employed both by the boss and by his opponents, the "mongrels." Beer parties and house parties are time-honored institutions. The beer parties are conducted in much the same way as the smoke talks already described. Tickets are issued, and sometimes two or three hundred attend. A beer party is held for the purpose of making the friends of the candidate "solid," and of gaining recruits. There are certain heelers and local leaders who figure largely at such times, and are known as "beer party orators." The speaking of the candidate and his friends amidst smoke, sandwiches, and beer, is always personal. The fact that the candidate is a "good fellow" is the chief theme. Issues are not referred to. The house party is a smaller gathering held at the home of the candidate early in the campaign. Those invited are principally his lieutenants. Invitations are issued, however, very seductively to the certain small leaders who are not "fixed" as yet. The strong camaraderie induced by the beer, sandwiches, and other refreshments, makes the planning which is done at such parties much more eager and effective. This social feeling creates temporarily a new gang with all its loyalties; for the sentiment is quite strong in these wards that those who attend such parties shall vote and work for the candidate giving them.

The ward committee usually indorses certain machine candidates before the caucus. This is not always done formally. Sometimes it is simply understood. The cause of such a candidate is then the cause of the boss. The system is of course unfair and undemocratic. In the caucus of the party, all men should be on an equality; none should be ticketed "regular," none "independent." The situation is, however, a natural result of gang rule. Let us assume that a man is running for office, — for the Massachusetts House of Representatives. This will help to bring out in clear relief the advantages possessed by the boss, and the impossibility to a respectable man, not a gang man and without gang connections, of overcoming the start of the machine-indorsed candidate. It takes four or five hundred votes to win a contest. In such wards there are from one hundred to three hundred City employees. Then there

are a large number of those who are "looking for
something." As a result, it would be impossible
for a man of strict honor to throw off such a handi-
cap, however able and genial a man he happened
to be. In an ethical calculation, those "dead
votes" do not count; in reality they count as much
as votes representing honest conviction. These
men vote as the boss wishes. Add to their votes
those of the men who can be bought with a drink,
or who can be falsely registered, — and from these
sources alone there are two or three hundred votes,
perhaps more. Every such corrupt vote neutral-
izes an honest one. In this analysis of machine
votes, we have not taken into account the " popularity votes." If the candidate has been the leader
of a gang from boyhood up, has graduated from
the grammar school, is a good fighter and a good
fellow, knows the social code of the saloon, and
has a dash of respectability in dress and appearance, — he is popular and a successful candidate.
In the candidates of these wards, personal popularity is almost essential; the question of fitness
for the office cuts little or no figure. Here again
the best men of the district must often meet failure.

The caucus is the scene where all this network
of social life and these various typical characters

in ward politics come fully into play. On entering
the caucus room at 7 P. M., one would see a line
stretching on two sides of the great hall and reaching into the street. Men fill the hall and the yard.
All along the line are the various lieutenants of
the different candidates peddling the tickets of
their favorites. The candidates themselves usually
stand in line where they can speak to their friends
and give them the " glad hand." All is noise and
action. Men push each other along the line in
good-natured rough fashion. The ticket peddlers
poke their cards into each successive face from
the gate to the rail, and loudly call the names of
their patrons. As the evening wears on, curious
yells are given for the popular candidates, an-
swered by cat-calls from the friends of their opponents. Perhaps a rough, jolly gang will throw up
some fellow into the air, and as he comes down
knock his hat in. Occasionally the disputes of
rival heelers will issue in a fight. All around, one
will see a fine assortment of " bums " going from
candidate to candidate and quietly " touching "
them for a half dollar, a quarter, or even the price
of a drink. To refuse is to be called a " hinge,"
—and stinginess is the most unpopular sin in the
ward. Young men with ball tickets, benefit tickets, and other such things to sell will also go from

candidate to candidate. To refuse to buy is dangerous. " Touching " is an art of which a caucus produces many devotees.

Heelers may be seen passing out to a neighboring saloon with a group of men, and sending them back to vote " right; " perhaps giving them tickets and a name to vote upon. There are many men who never attend a caucus. Their names repeaters can use with little fear of detection. Frequently the right of a repeater to vote is loudly challenged by the opponents of the machine. Then there is an excited rush to the rail. As a rule, the warden, all powerful, only turns his back, or smiles sardonically.[1]

In this boisterous crowd the boss walks as a petty sovereign. In close contests he has, of course, all the machinery described, social and political, in good working order. He is there now to put into execution plans already made, and to meet " emergencies." Occasionally he stands near the entrance of the booths scanning each passing voter, smiling and chatty, or scowling and gruff, always masterful, hypnotizing many men into doing his bidding when they had otherwise made

[1] It must be remembered that at times the caucus is very "harmonious," — when the boss has disposed of all opposition in advance.

up their minds. In meeting candidates opposing those of his choice, he jokes with them or looks at them witheringly, as serves his purpose. If his opponent has brought out a new worker, he usually seeks an introduction, smiling and affable. Occasionally in a close contest he calls some effective worker of his opponent aside and makes him a tempting offer, provided he will get "suddenly sick" and drop out of the game. Such an offer is carefully adapted to suit the case in hand. The boss tries to keep posted on the "wants" of each man. It is important information in the complications of ward politics.

In the course of the evening a repeater may be arrested. As the man is hurried out of the place, a great crowd following, the lieutenant of the boss runs to the police station to "make it all right," or to go bail. In the mean time, the boss finds the "informer," and before an admiring and much impressed crowd denounces him for "swearing away a man's liberty." His tones are so dramatic, so earnest, so morally indignant, that faces quite unused to seriousness look ludicrously grave and convinced. It is pure buncombe, but the boss knows his audience; he gains many votes to compensate for his slight loss.

If it happen to be a caucus in which the oppo-

sition grows stronger and stronger, he may be
seen darting here and there holding excited con-
versations with some local leader or with one of
his own workers, or perhaps sending some heeler
to secure more voters or engage a noted repeater.
"Bums," the semi-criminal class, his own immediate and more respectable followers, are all in
the caucus room ready to be manipulated at any
such crisis in whatsoever way seems to him best.

At last the hurly-burly's done; and the boss
can look forward again to long months of peaceful
possession. Most of those who have ventured to
oppose him will soon seek his favor. Breaches of
any consequence will quickly be healed; and the
united strength of a dominant party will again,
as always before, make the final election to office
mere dumb show.

This unconscionable affair — which occurs at a
point within fifteen minutes' walk of the Public
Library and Trinity Church — is thus at once the
climax and the résumé of local politics. It is calculated to arouse sombre reflections; for under
the American system, the primary election is the
nestling-place of our liberties.

# CHAPTER VII

## CRIMINAL TENDENCIES

In the district covered by these chapters, crime outright consists almost wholly of isolated offenses. These are not confined to any one locality or section, but may happen anywhere throughout the entire district. In the South Cove even, with its traditions of lawlessness, crime is hardly more frequent than elsewhere. Indeed, there are to-day no criminal centres in the South End. Broadly speaking, life and property are as safe in one part as in another.

To be sure, there are not wanting neighborhoods which would seem to furnish the right background for deeds of violence, with their courts of tall buildings into whose rooms but little sunshine ever finds its way; their blind alleys with dwellings in all stages of dilapidation; and an occasional single house so shut in on all sides by high blank walls, that were it at the bottom of some cañon its isolation and gloom could hardly be greater. But these in many cases have known no darker drama than that of human wretchedness and despair.

Not only are there no nests of crime in this district, but scattered criminal deeds of any serious nature are comparatively infrequent. The shooting of a man as the result of a quarrel, the murder of a woman by her husband in a drunken rage, the killing of a man on account of jealousy, and two or three murderous assaults with intent to rob comprise the sum of those within the past three or four years. Minor crimes, however, are not uncommon, the most frequent of these being robbery of some kind. Small boys, usually in gangs, pilfer wherever they can, especially from vacant buildings. Older thieves snatch pocket-books on the streets; and sneak into hallways and rooms for whatever they can find. There is but little breaking and entering, partly because the crowded population makes this difficult, and partly because such a quarter offers few inducements to the professional burglar.

Some idea of the extent of crime in this district may be had from the number of arrests made here in one year. The district falls within two police divisions, the Boston and Albany Railroad, which cuts it in two unequally, forming the dividing line between them. There were arrested by

the police of Station 5 in 1897, 3625 persons; and
by the police of Station 4, which covers many
downtown streets, 6636 persons. By a careful
estimate, one third of the former number and one
fourth of the latter resided within our district.
No less than 2800 persons living in this part of
the South End, therefore, were arrested during
that year. As one would expect, the great majority of these were arrested for drunkenness.
The number of arrests throughout both police
divisions for larceny was 469; for assault, 528;
breaking and entering, 72; and malicious mischief, 42. The district under review, it should be
remembered, covers only about half the territory
included within these two police divisions.

Comparatively free as the district is from crimes
of the more serious kind, it is nevertheless infested
by suspicious characters of all sorts. The number
of such persons arrested by the police of the two
stations during 1896 was 520, a good proportion
of whom, it may be assumed, were arrested within
our bounds. Why so many lawbreakers of one
kind and another should resort here, while their
fields of operation are elsewhere, is explained by
the general accessibility of the district, by its nearness on the northern side to great railroad termi-
nals, and by its many lodging houses of the lower

grade in which concealment is so easy. Naturally more of this class are to be found in the immediate neighborhood of the railroad stations than elsewhere. Albany, Hudson, and Tyler streets are especially frequented by them.

All the wrongdoers to be found in the district, however, are not mere sojourners in it. Not a few belong here. The number of men and women who have "done time," chiefly for drunkenness or disorderliness, is very large. A straggling procession of such offenders, with an occasional thief or murderer, is continually passing to and fro between this part of the city and the various penal institutions. As a consequence, a sentence to a term of imprisonment affects but little one's standing in his own estimation or in that of his circle of friends and acquaintances. The offender looks upon himself, and is looked upon, as merely unfortunate. He fell into the hands of the law while others equally culpable escaped, — that is all. Not infrequently his mishap is a subject of jest to himself and his acquaintances. He is "going into the country," if sentenced to the inebriate hospital at Foxboro or to the reformatory at Concord; or "going to the seashore" if sent to the House of Correction on Deer Island. There is often, of course, some sense of shame on the culprit's part, but a sense of contrition is rare.

The presence of so many resident offenders cannot be accounted for so easily as that of the floating lawbreakers. Central situation, contiguity to railroad stations, lodging houses, will not explain it. It is due in large part to the social conditions that exist here. There are tenement courts in which the dense crowding of the poorest people of all sorts, resulting in lack of individual or even family privacy, absence of anything like decent standards of living, familiarity with debasing sights and sounds, and contact with the vicious and depraved, induces, if it does not compel, the development of the worst morbid tendencies. A child born in such a place is almost predestined to a vicious if not criminal life.

Beside the immediate conditions which foster the " microbe of criminality," there are many and varied agencies of evil which furnish further incitement. Many of the billiard and pool rooms are centres of such influence. Here the baser sort congregate, and exchange the latest criminal news and the gossip of the underworld. But the pool rooms are a less serious source of corruption than they would be if there were bars in connection with them. Happily a police regulation forbids the sale of liquor in these places. In not a few instances, however, they are next door to saloons.

Besides the saloon, which affects fully half the local families as a baneful agency, the cheap theatres are injurious, less because of the plays they present than because of the kind of person that loiters about them.

The real degradation of this district, then, consists far less in the crimes, great and small, committed here, or in the lawbreakers of various kinds and degrees that resort here, than in the existence of conditions and of agencies which make crime easy and fascinating, and virtue hard and unattractive, for the people in general. Comparatively unproductive of graver crime, the district is most prolific in vice and immorality. Drunkenness and prostitution flourish rankly. Both are involved together with crime, but each has also an existence more or less by itself.

Gambling, which usually is associated with all these, has been reduced in the South End, by police vigilance, almost to the vanishing point. Boys match pennies, negroes indulge on the sly in policy, and the Chinese play fan tan. With these exceptions there is now but little gambling aside from playing for drinks in pool rooms and saloons. Nearly all the arrests for this offense are among the Chinese, who are brought to Station 4 in groups of from two or three to twenty or more.

Gambling is so much a part of the life of that race that it cannot easily be dislodged from among them. While the Chinese remain here, patrol wagons filled with them will continue to drive up to the police stations.

The number of places where liquor licenses are held varies year by year. In 1897 it was almost exactly two hundred, including groceries, whole-sale liquor establishments, restaurants, and saloons. About one hundred of them were ordinary bar-rooms. This, it should be remembered, is in an area of less than three quarters of a square mile.

Besides the licensed places for the sale of liquor there is a considerable number of resorts where it is sold illegally. These are called "speak easies." How numerous they are cannot be determined. Unquestionably, however, their number has decreased since the appearance of the saloon-hotel, with its special privilege of selling liquor after eleven at night, and on Sundays and holidays, — the very times when the "speak easies" do their best business. To be sure, the sale of liquors out of saloon hours by the saloon-hotel must be in connection with meals, but these need consist of nothing more than a piece of bread. Competing with the unlicensed bar-rooms as it does, along their own lines, the saloon-hotel must have the effect of pushing them to the wall. Wherever liquor is now sold surreptitiously it is for the most part merely an accompaniment of worse things.

As one would infer from the number and variety of drinking-places, the liquor habit, in some degree, is very general throughout this section. In certain neighborhoods it is practically universal among both men and women. Women, however, are forbidden by police regulation to patronize the bar-rooms. To avoid the offense of turning would-be customers away, some of the saloons display the sign, "No drinks sold to ladies." In a very large number of cases drinking is excessive. There were arrested for drunkenness in 1897 by the police of the two stations covering our district 6960 persons, one third of them undoubtedly living within the district's limits. When it is remembered that only the more troublesome drunkards are arrested, some idea will be had of the amount of intoxication that exists here.

As to the causes of drunkenness, so far as they can be got at, some act here as they act everywhere, and some are involved in local conditions.

Chief of the general causes is the craving for excitement. The poor man drinks in the midst of his lack, just as the rich man drinks in the

midst of his surfeit.    Both, in the ordinary round
of their lives, seek a stimulus to lift them out of
their inertia.    Social instinct also leads the way
to intoxication.    In addition to these influences, no
doubt a large amount of drinking may be traced
directly to morbid appetite, induced by immorality
of different sorts.

Of the causes operative here and not everywhere, poverty easily comes first.    Drink and poverty have a complicated reciprocal bearing on each
other.    Poor food, insanitary surroundings, mean
homes, lead to drink; and in turn follow from
drink.    The saloon rises out of conditions that
poverty furnishes, and at the same time perpetu-
ates those conditions.

If one of the results of poverty is a more fertile source of drunkenness than another, it is the
absence of resource in the poor man's life.    Under
the stress of mood or emergency, the rich man has
many ways of escape.    The poor man has almost
no means but drink for establishing a counter-cur-
rent to any emotion that may strongly possess
him.    He drinks, therefore, in times of sorrow and
in times of joy, when overtaken by adversity and
when visited by prosperity.    Drink is his easiest
and most direct way over the restraints of his
narrow and hard lot.

Crime and drink are bound up together in somewhat the same way as poverty and drink. The criminal drinks because he represents a low grade of physical being ; and through drink he becomes the more hopelessly criminal. But the abuse of alcohol is by no means universal among the criminal class, especially where success depends on cleverness.

Drink is often not at all involved with either poverty or crime. Here as elsewhere it is bound in with social custom, and casual acquaintances resort to the saloon as a matter of course. The saloon as a club for certain gangs has already been mentioned. In general it undertakes to be a club merely in the restricted sense of having, in many cases, a tolerably well-defined group of patrons, who come to have certain privileges. With a few exceptions the saloons provide no seats. Most of them have but limited free space outside the bar. Loitering here after the drink is finished is not encouraged. Indeed, the loafer will be invited to give way to new arrivals. In the case of the poor man the street is his hospitable club rather than the saloon. Here he will meet his companions, resorting to the saloon for drinking only. There are two or three German saloons that provide chairs and tables, and here men may pass the entire evening over their beer, papers, and games. But the constituency of these resorts is necessarily limited. The gilded saloon, with its welcoming warmth, its cheery light, and other enticements, where, for the price of two or three glasses of liquor, the poor man may pass an evening with boon companions, hardly exists in the district.

The reason for this is the necessity of good order imposed by the Board of Police ; and as all screens are forbidden, every passing citizen is in effect a police officer. Under this same constraint, the saloon does not in every case use all possible means to increase its trade. While it may resort to various devices for drawing men in, as the free lunch, pugilistic news, and baseball returns, yet there are instances where it intentionally cuts down the sale of liquor. It is somewhat surprising to find that a sedative is not infrequently given, unknown to the customer, to lessen the morbid craving. There is a firm that has the curious business of manufacturing such a sedative, which it sells in large quantities to saloon - keepers throughout the city. Some saloons, also, apparently do not try to force their trade much beyond the demand already existing in their immediate neighborhoods.

Far more serious than drunkenness is the shadowy but ever-present curse of prostitution. It is much more deeply rooted in the South End than in any other part of the city. The most casual observer cannot fail to detect some signs of its presence. He might not see any direct solicitation on the street; but his attention would be drawn toward certain young women with something in their manner or dress calculated to attract notice. Usually two of these go together. Sometimes they hurry on as though intent on reaching their destination in the briefest time possible; they brush against the passers-by, and respond with a careless laugh or pert remark to any chance greeting. At other times they saunter along seemingly engaged in earnest conversation with each other, but quick to catch one's eye and to greet effusively whoever may address them.

These young women represent only one grade of the general class to which they belong. Even since becoming members of the underworld they have seen more prosperous days, and have gravitated down to a lower plane in their erring, sorrowful persuasion. In almost every case they are beginning to suffer the extreme consequences of their manner of life. Some of these women disappear from the district after a time, only to re-

appear months later. They are said to travel on
a regular circuit, stopping in a place for a few
months or until they become known to the police.

Above the level of the woman of the street are
those who promote their calling in private and by
indirect means; and there is a still higher grade
made up of women who are not married to the
men with whom they associate, but for the time at
least are faithful to them. Then there are not
wanting abandoned types still lower than the ordinary woman of the street, who frequent the cheapest eating-places and kitchen bar-rooms, and wait
at the doors of the meanest saloons; or prowl
around docks and marshes in company with sailors
and tramps.

Estimates as to the number of this general
class, even at the lowest, are sufficiently startling.
From the very nature of the case, however, these
estimates must be very largely a matter of opinion.
The line of demarcation which separates this class
from the rest of the community is of course somewhat indefinite; and in most cases it would be a
matter of much difficulty to identify the individual
members of the class. All that can be said as to
the number of women in this part of the city living
in illicit relations is that it is large and constitutes not an inconsiderable fraction of the local

population. It would be more difficult still to give any sort of estimate as to the number of the men who are more or less involved. They come from all classes in the community. It is likely, indeed, that these unrecognized accomplices of the " social evil " stand in somewhat the same proportion to the population in every section of the city as the women culprits represent in the South End.

Another sign of this evil is the number and appearance of the hotels of the district. These hotels, more numerous than one would expect in a section of this kind, are quiet during the day and apparently almost deserted ; but as evening comes on they undergo a marked change. Office and bar-room begin to fill up. Parties of men and women arrive on foot or in carriages with increasing frequency. As late as midnight, and well into the morning, the places are brightly lighted from top to bottom.

According to report and outward evidence, the larger number of these hotels are, to a greater or less extent, places of assignation. Women frequent the supper rooms, where they are known to be present and can easily be sought; and hither resort women and men in company. From time to time these hotels are the scene of unimaginable revels. When one of them becomes too notorious it is suppressed for a time. It soon opens again, however, with some change of front, but the same real character. None of the leading hotels in the district has kept the same name for any considerable length of time.

A tendency on the part of the saloons to change into small hotels has already been spoken of. Each year of late has added to the list of these saloon-hotels, although at present the policy of the Board of Police seems to be to restrict their increase. Certainly in many cases the returns from the additional liquor privilege are not sufficient to justify the maintenance of the number of rooms required by a hotel license. Neither can the cafés, with one or two exceptions, be an important source of income. Of ordinary hotel constituency, there is practically none, so far as this district is concerned.

There is one almost weird aspect of this degraded life, which has already been suggested in the previous chapter.[1] Here and there in doorways and on street corners one will notice a young man and woman, each having distinctive characteristics, talking earnestly together. Often the girl seems to be pleading with her companion. The young man represents that most detestable type, the

[1] See pages 122, 131.

"lover." Wherever prostitution prevails, this type
will always be found. It results, undoubtedly,
from the desire of even the most abandoned woman to have some one man's special regard. The
"lover" exercises something of authority and even
terrorism over his mistress. He compels her to
contribute to his support, while he idles away
much of his time in pool rooms and saloons.
Until recently the headquarters of the "lovers"
of our district was a pool room on Washington
Street, where a group could be seen at almost any
time of the day or evening.

Not the least pointed indications of prostitution
are the frequent signs, massage, manicure, clair-
voyant, and even millinery or dressmaking. In
many instances such signs are, without doubt, honest advertisements, but not in all. An investigation instituted not long ago by an experienced
social worker disclosed the fact, that in some
instances, at least, these were merely the cipher
signs of immorality. In some of the places visited, — which had been selected as the most suspicious, — there was no pretense whatever of carrying on the business advertised, and the ulterior
motive was found to be really the only one.

Solicitation is not confined to such places. It
occurs on the street, but usually in ways so subtle

as to escape the ordinary observer. In some quarters, however, it is so open and bold that it could hardly fail to be noticed by any one. Until recently one passing along a certain street would hear voices behind the blinds of nearly every house, inviting him to enter. In another street, equally open solicitation is still made.

So much for the more direct and obvious way of observing the evil of prostitution in the district under review. We can approach it on quite different sides by means of the police records and medical reports of the district. While the observer might see it on the side of its morbid fascination, these data present its revolting outcome. In 1897 the police of Stations 4 and 5 made 243 arrests for offenses, more or less heinous, coming under this general head; a large proportion of these presumably in our district. The medical reports bear witness to the ramifying effects of this curse, through showing the prevalence of diseases directly traceable to it.

From whichever side we approach prostitution in our district, we are impressed by its magnitude. It is not too much to say that it has its haunts throughout the length and breadth of the district. No section or neighborhood — one might almost say, no block — is free from it. And yet, notwithstanding that it is so widespread, the burden and horror of it might be somewhat alleviated, did it not stand for every sort of perversion of rudimentary feeling and instinct. St. Paul's description of the complexity of immorality in the heathen world might be applied with the utmost literalness, word by word, and phrase by phrase, to this district.

The aggregate enormity of all this, while it may continue to excite our wonder, will cause less surprise as we study the district itself. It is, to begin with, a natural meeting place. Then its traditions are on the side of moral laxity. Formerly for a period of years this district was left pretty much to its own devices. All sorts of evils flourished here with but little interference from any source. The lower half of the South End was regarded as a kind of moral waste. All this is now much changed, but the tradition remains. Immorality still persists in expecting to be freer from molestation here than elsewhere.

Still deeper reasons for the strong local intrenchment of prostitution and all that is akin to it are to be found in local social conditions. Here is a dense lodging-house and tenement-house population representing all nationalities and every grade of middle-class and working-class existence.

A large proportion of this population consists of unattached individuals, free from the usual restraints of family and community life, and having, in many cases, but the most meagre resources to draw upon for recreation and entertainment.

Some tenement-house quarters, especially inducive to crime, are at the same time rife with certain forms of immorality. Tenement-house life, in general, — except in tenements of the highest grade, — can hardly escape what is mean and low. In many cases, the familiarity shown by children of the tenements with wrongdoing of all descriptions is extremely shocking. The horror of this would be lessened were not the children always liable to become to the full extent the victims of the conditions under which they are condemned to live. Girls of tender years are lured into a life of shame. Boys come to man's estate with their whole nature corrupted and ruined. Drink, in adult life, is the fatal logic of such an adolescence.

Lodging houses also, in a different way, constitute a fertile soil for all this noxious growth. The variety of people thrown together promiscuously in lodging houses is a matter of constant surprise. For instance, in a house of about an average grade there were at one time: a hus-

band and wife, the former a professional spiritualist, the latter a lecturer for a prominent temperance organization; a woman with a son who
attended the high school during the day and in
the evening acted as usher in a leading theatre; a
workman in a laundry; a bartender; and a news-
paper reporter. The woman who kept the house,
although a loose character, was very active in temperance work.

The lodgers need not have much to do with one
another, or even know each other; but the very
freedom of lodging-house relations is very likely
to result in relaxed morals. The almost universal
absence of a common parlor where the lodgers
may receive their visitors, especially those of the
opposite sex; and the lack, in general, of suitable
provision for the reserves and proprieties of life,
tend still more to break down social and moral
barriers.

Three types of lodging houses may be distinguished: those where every sort of irregularity
goes on, but in an unorganized way; those outwardly respectable, but sheltering more or less
wrongdoing within; and those that are truly respectable.

A house of the first type furnishes temporary
shelter to the wholly irresponsible, if not criminal,

element in the district. Visitors arrive and depart at any hour of the day or night. Men and women lodgers pass in and out of each others' rooms indifferently. If it is of the lowest grade, Negroes and white people may be found lodging under the same roof. A house of this class is not infrequently the scene of robbery and sometimes of murder. This and the seemingly respectable type of houses are perhaps the most numerous, but the third class is well represented. All the houses of this class, even, are not always free from wrongdoing, notwithstanding the vigilance of those keeping them. Indeed, there are relatively few lodging houses in the entire district upon which the shadow of suspicion never falls.

As to organized houses of prostitution in this district it is difficult to speak with exactness. Undoubtedly they exist, but police vigilance is diminishing their number and is leading those which still remain to observe order and seek obscurity. Whole streets once given over to such houses have been recovered by the police. Within a few years one of the most notorious streets in the South End has been completely transformed ; and it is now, under a new name, quiet and law-abiding. More recently the houses of another such street have been broken up and their inmates scattered through this and other parts of the South End.

It is curious to note that after a neighborhood has been cleared of the haunts of evil, its houses, after remaining vacant for a time, gradually fill up with Jews, for the most part. This may be easily accounted for by the depreciated rents of the vacated houses and by the indifference of the Jews to the reputation of the locality where they live. There are instances where Jews and Negroes occupy the same houses in some of these reclaimed neighborhoods.

Like most great poor quarters, the district under observation has developed a Bowery of its own, around which centre the excitements of vice. Those who come into the district to do wrong undoubtedly come first of all to the theatres, small dime museums, and other places of amusement along Washington Street. These, together with the saloons, pool rooms, all-night restaurants, and all the excitements of this street, give the fascinations of vice their full chance. When the work of the day is over, crowds of pleasure seekers fill the sidewalks; hotels and theatres become brilliant with lights; the hurdy-gurdy jingles merrily; and the street is changed for a time into a sort of fair, where evil offers itself in many attractive guises. The spectacular nature of its great thoroughfare is to the district a source of incitement to vice.

As long, therefore, as the South End remains what it is, — accessible, congested, overshadowed by its past, having its lingering crowds and its great amusement resorts, — prostitution will certainly be rampant here. Police raids may break up its organized centres, dislodge it from this or that haunt, and effect a change in its method ; but they are not able to stamp it out, or even greatly to diminish it. And yet raiding is by no means futile. It pushes prostitution into the background and prevents it from flaunting itself boldly and defiantly in the face of all. What is of more importance, however, it inspires the inhabitants of the underworld, through a wholesome fear of the law, with a feeling of insecurity in their abandoned course. An evil that every moment is fearful of attack fails of many of its worst results.

So much for the criminal tendencies of the district as a whole. There are certain aspects of crime and immorality as seen in the district which go with different industrial and racial groups. The economic bearing of these things is important, though elusive. The relation between poverty and drink has been touched upon. There is a gradation of crime on the basis of skill. The unskilled labor class will develop here and there a burly ruffian. The housebreaker must almost necessarily be a mechanic. The clerk purloins or falsifies his accounts or forges his employer's name. Among women the several different types of prostitution represent the different industrial grades. The lower types are recruited predominantly from the inferior ranks of women's labor, domestic service especially; the higher types, which include a smaller number, from store and office employment. The source of evil, from the economic point of view, is that the woman, like the rest of the world, seeks a higher standard of freedom and opportunity than that which she has. There are doubtless occasional instances in which women are practically driven into sin by want; but these are rare. The more common case is almost as pathetic, — where wages are less than five dollars a week and about four dollars is pledged in advance for board and lodging. It is certain that a very frequent motive is the love of excitement, luxury, and indolence; but there are many times when the downward step means only that the human spirit refuses to be held to the limits of bare subsistence.

All of the tendencies described in this chapter

are not to be found among each of the great racial groups of the district; nor in the same degree in any two of them. Drunkenness, for instance, is the great sin of the Irish population. The use of liquors, of one kind or another, may be more general in some other nationality than the Irish; but intoxication is a marked trait of theirs. The number of Irish arrested for drunkenness and the misdemeanors and offenses growing directly out of drunkenness, is relatively far greater than that of any other nationality. On the other hand, the Irish women maintain the high standard of chastity which is the distinction of their race. This may be traced directly to the influence of the Catholic Church, — especially of the confessional. Comparatively few among them turn to a dissolute life.

The Jews are conspicuously free from the vice of intemperance and from sins against the family; but in the case of the Russian Jews, who largely predominate in the Hebrew section of the district, they are extremely quarrelsome among themselves. No class here gives the police so much petty annoyance as do the Russian Jews. They run to the police station on the slightest provocation to enter complaints against the offending parties, offering to verify their charges by producing witnesses to any desired number. There is a widespread suspicion in police circles that the prospect on the part of the observers of securing witness fees is often oil to the fires of contention.

While the Negroes are peaceable, and on the whole temperate, their licentiousness is notorious. In many cases family lines seem to be almost obliterated. Gambling is only a less conspicuous vice among them, and pilfering is by no means uncommon.

A high type of good order is represented by the people from the British Provinces; although it is somewhat startling to find that the ranks of prostitution are to a considerable degree recruited from among them.

Notwithstanding the marked and widespread criminal tendencies of the district, declaring themselves even in an occasional serious crime, it is nevertheless far from being lawless or turbulent. One who does not go out of his way to give offense can visit even the worst neighborhoods without suffering molestation or insult. The well-behaved are everywhere let alone, if not respected. There are some hoodlums, but they rarely manifest themselves as such.

Of course the tenements are more or less noisy, and drunken brawls are not infrequent in them;

but besides the noise and quarreling there is comparatively little real disorder. When the number of drinking places is taken into account, the number of drunkards on the streets is comparatively small. Rarely is there a street fight of any consequence; mob violence is unknown. A case of holding up and robbing some belated pedestrian is reported now and then, but not more frequently here than in more favored parts of the city.

This general orderliness and safety is due very largely, without doubt, to the vigilance of the police; but it is due also in no small degree to the character of the people themselves. The Irishman may drink and quarrel, but he is first and last chivalrous, and will intercede to protect the weak from the oppression of the strong; the Russian Jew, whatever bickerings he may have with his neighbors, seldom goes far beyond the bounds of law and order; and the Negro, loose as he is in character, is usually gentle enough at heart.

But the district has not always been as it is now in respect to law and order. Not so many years ago lawlessness was far greater, especially in the region of the South Cove. The change for the better, year after year, has been brought about chiefly by effective police administration. Notorious gangs that once terrorized certain localities have been broken up; old offenders have been driven away or placed under close surveillance; concealment has been made more difficult; the illegal sale of liquors lessened; and prostitution driven further and further under cover. The improvement still goes on. Each year finds the district a little more orderly, — at least in its outward aspects, — a little freer from the graver crimes, a little less open in its vices. Just how far this movement in the direction of law and order will be able to carry us, cannot be predicted. But when the law has done its utmost, however free the district may be from all other manifestations of criminal tendencies, it will still remain overshadowed by drunkenness and prostitution. The combined influence of all helpful social effort in the district must be depended upon for deeper and further results. It may as well be said in advance, however, that there is no organized force yet in evidence which, even were its possibilities exhausted, would be equal to these dark and tragic evils.

# CHAPTER VIII

OF all the places of amusement at the South
End there was none so popular locally, and so interesting and typical in itself, as the old Grand
Dime Museum, at the chief corner of the district,
where Dover Street crosses Washington. As it
was before the changes made in 1896, by which it
became the new Grand Theatre, it introduced, or
shall we say preserved, a certain old-time atmosphere in the midst of the prevailing commonplace-
ness. The scenes presented upon its stage, the
audience lost in the story enacted, seemed like
bits of Dickens — incidents and characters out of
those chapters in the book of life which he made
so completely his own. Little imagination was
needed to give to it all a reality and naturalness
which has been lost in the "improvements" of
the past two years. There was a certain quality
in the plays to be enjoyed even by a person accustomed to higher types of amusement. The tragedy
was lurid, the comedy coarse, there was much to

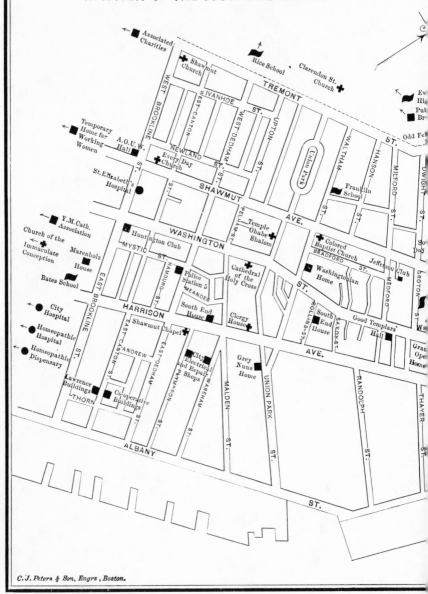

MAP TO SHOW THE
CHIEF INSTITUTIONS & MEETING PLACES
IN A PART OF THE SOUTH END BOSTON

C. J. Peters & Son, Engrs , Boston.

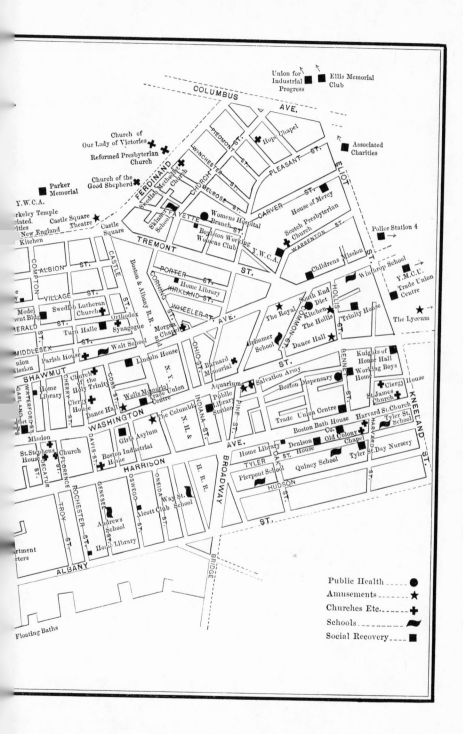

grate upon fine sensibilities; but there was withal back of it the red blood of the simpler human feelings and passions, that made good a multitude of faults. The audiences applauded the brave lover, devoted wife, and fond mother; hissed the villain and rejoiced in his downfall. There might be absence of good taste, but there was plenty of evidence that the heart was right.

The old building in which the Grand Dime was located has had an interesting history. Once known as the Windsor Theatre, it later became the headquarters of the Salvation Army, and ten years ago it came under the control of the present owner. Under his management the theatre has proved exceedingly successful financially, and it has been really useful as a purveyor of amusement to the people of the South End and of South Boston. It is the great popular resort for these two large sections. Every boy and man, many of the girls, and some of the women, regard an afternoon or an evening at the Dime now and then as an indispensable part of their lives. The Dime is to them what the theatre, the opera, and the symphony are to the more fortunate classes in the community. It is the only means by which they can obtain the enjoyment that is derived from the imagination. That the craving is strong is shown by the crowded houses always to be seen at this resort.

The performance begins promptly at one o'clock with variety features. At two o'clock the drama opens. Interspersed between the acts is the " olio," consisting of a number of variety exhibits, musical, humorous, sleight-of-hand, ventriloquist, and athletic. The same performance is repeated in the evening, beginning at seven. A single play with its accompanying vaudeville features is given usually for a week ; then there is a complete change of bill and frequently of actors as well. The same management has under its control two theatres in other parts of Boston, and theatres at four smaller New England cities. In 1896 it had ten stock companies and a star company. The star company, besides playing at the home houses, toured through the country.

Overwrought melodrama has all along had probably the chief popularity at the Dime, although its reign is not quite so assured as it once was. The startling situations, the portrayal of forceful human sentiments and passions, thrill the people and satisfy their demand for strong colors and broad effects. The manager says that there is now, however, more demand for frequent change in the kind of amusement. Formerly for week

after week the people were content with the melodrama. They never seemed to tire of it. Now
they demand an occasional society play with its
pictures of a life so different from their own.
Comedy, especially of the Celtic kind, has always
had a prominent place in the programmes.

Many of the plays have been the standard and
popular dramas that are usually no longer given in
other theatres. The old favorites, like " The Two
Orphans " and " East Lynne," regularly reappear
at the Dime now that they have become too thread-
bare for the higher priced houses. The plays are
touched up to suit the preferences of the people.
The ghost is introduced in " Dr. Jekyll and Mr.
Hyde," in order to make clear how the victim
haunts the murderer. Local hits and popular
" gags " are brought in. Passing incidents or well-
known personalities are used as subjects of remark.
All these efforts meet with ready appreciation on
the part of the listeners. The nearer home such
allusions come, the better they are liked; for the
people, with all their love of the romantic, the sen-
timental, and the improbable, enjoy best of all a
presentation of these features of existence with
which they are familiar. The vagaries of a drunken
man, the follies of an Irish servant girl, the ex-
ploits of a policeman, and other scenes from street

and tenement-house life are always and everywhere hailed with loud applause. The people are at heart realists, whatever else they may be now and then. Like all the rest of us, they measure the world of the imagination by the narrow range of their own little sphere; just as did the poor woman who, on being shown the picture of a fateful scene in the French Revolution, thought it must be an eviction. The apparently morbid taste of an audience like that of the Dime for the pathetic — the family stricken with grief or distressed by want, the betrayed girl, the honest man wronged by some upstart superior — is really the natural outcome of the kind of experience with which their round of life makes them only too familiar.

In the spring of 1896 the old Grand Dime closed its doors to allow for extensive improvements. An enlarged gallery was provided for the patrons at the lowest prices. The old gallery had been the great refuge for those who had only a dime to spare for their amusement. Boys and men especially frequented it, and it has probably furnished enjoyment to more people than any similar place in Boston. It was by far the most characteristic part of the old Grand Dime. Its associations, indeed, were like those of the pit in olden times. The scene in the gallery on a Saturday or a Monnight, when some thrilling melodrama or an Irish comedy held the boards, was one long to be remembered. Every seat was taken, and every inch of standing room. An experienced observer, running his eye over the gallery, could pick out the various classes of the people. The corner loafer, the out-of-work, the casual laborer, the mechanic, and the clerk were all there. The few classes unrepresented in the gallery were to be found in other parts of the house, — the cheap and flashy aristocracy in the boxes, the respectability of the district in the seats on the orchestra floor. On such a night one got at the Dime a cross-section of the population of the district.

In August, 1896, the house reopened as the New Grand Theatre. In appearance it is at least cleaner. The dingy old walls have been showily decorated, and an attempt has been made to improve the ventilation. There is a new drop curtain on which is painted a picture of the bridge over the pond in the Public Garden, with one of the familiar swan-boats in the foreground. An advertisement occupies a conspicuous place in the middle of the curtain. The exterior of the building has been painted white, and numerous electric-light letters on the front of it fill the street with their glare at night.

Among the bills offered since the reopening have been "Dr. Jekyll and Mr. Hyde," "A Celebrated Case," "Outcasts of a Great City," "The Two Orphans," "The Clemenceau Case," "Little Hurricane," "Temptation of Money," "The Brand of Cain." Each week there has been a full vaudeville programme. The admission prices remain practically unchanged from those of the old Dime days. They are ten cents for the gallery, twenty cents for the balcony, twenty-five cents for the orchestra, and fifty cents for a box seat.

The feeling of the management seems to be that the programmes presented here have been improved to the same extent as the building. There is greater variety, and better known plays have at times been given; but to one who was fond of the old place there is a great void. The vulgarity of the performance is no longer relieved by picturesque features. Imitation of the higher priced theatres has taken the place of the originality of other days. Dickens land is lost to the South End by the transformation of the old Dime into the New Grand. The crowded houses each week would seem to indicate popular approval. The observer, however, has a secret feeling of regret; and regret may turn to revulsion, especially as there is at present a tendency toward low burlesque.

Next to the Grand Theatre in importance as a popular resort is its imposingly named rival, the Grand Opera House, on Washington Street, only a few steps further on from the corner of Dover. The building was intended for a high-class theatre, but its situation has prevented it from competing successfully with houses more conveniently placed. After various vicissitudes it passed in March, 1896, into the hands of Chicago men, who opened it as a popular amusement place with low prices, — ten, twenty, and thirty cents. The new managers had gained experience in conducting an exceedingly successful popular theatre in Chicago. Their success there led them to open the Grand Opera as an amusement place of a similar kind. Their theory, as expressed by the business manager, was that the drama draws the women, and the variety the men. By including the two in the programme a pleasing combination, and an exhaustive, is easily effected.

There was a permanent stock company of about twelve leading members, a few of whom have played with good companies. Some of the plays given were, " My Partner," " The Ensign," " Galley Slave," " Jim the Penman," " Mr. Barnes of New York," " All the Comforts of Home," " Hazel Kirke," " Rooms for Rent," " The Vendetta,"

"Wife for Wife," "Taken from Life," "Our Boys." Many of these plays, so the management claimed, had never been given at such low prices before. As at the Grand Theatre, the bill was changed every week. There were two performances daily, from one to five o'clock in the afternoon, and from seven to half past ten in the evening. Beginning at two and at half past seven, the drama was given, the intervals before and between the acts being filled by vaudeville specialties. This house claimed to give an entertainment expressly suited to women and children. One of its announcements declared that it was the home of refined vaudeville and drama. Another placard stated that every day was a "bargain day." The theatre has unusually large capacity, accommodating about three thousand people. The management claimed good success from the beginning. Early in their first season, they estimated their audiences as ranging from twelve to fourteen thousand a week. It was nothing unusual to have over twelve hundred in the gallery alone. Of course with the large capacity of "the Opera," half a houseful was double the number that could possibly get into the Grand Dime in the old days. At the same time, the running expenses of the larger theatre would be considerably greater.

At the end of a year a change of management occurred. The same system of combined drama and vaudeville was continued, although innovations in mechanical effects were promised. The now well-known "moving pictures" in the form of the cinematograph proved to be the chief novelty of the management. After a brief season the house was closed for the summer. In September, 1897, the Grand Opera House experienced still another change of management. Another effort was made to return to the original plan of a high-priced theatre depending for its patronage upon the wider public of the city and the suburbs. The idea of a theatre with popular prices, furnishing amusement for the people of the district, was definitely abandoned. This last policy has been continued with moderate success up to the present.

The change is to be regretted, for the plan of a popular amusement resort, with prices suited to the resources of the people of the district, seems much more practicable than the one which had been originally tried. The location is a favorable one for a popular resort. Three theatres, the Grand, the Grand Opera, and the Columbia, are all within a short distance of each other. During the winter transient shows make their appearance in vacant stores near by. Here are grouped together the chief amusements of the South End. Here in the future will be the great centre of amusement for that "city of the poor" which is rapidly forming at the South End. Here the People's Palace of Pleasure and Delight must be reared. The imperfect beginnings of such a palace are to be found in the three theatres just mentioned, — business enterprises for the making of profit out of the craving for amusement in a people who have little enough with which to give life its essential gayety and joy.

Like the Grand Opera, the Columbia Theatre was intended to be a first-class theatre, but its situation has interfered with its success. Residents of the Back Bay and the suburbs can hardly be induced to come to the South End for their amusement ; and the people of the district cannot afford to pay the price required to support a high-class theatre. Therefore, after various experiments and several failures, it was found necessary to cater to the local district rather than to try unsuccessfully to attract hither the residents of remoter districts. The failure of the Grand Opera and the Columbia to succeed as first-class theatres illustrates very forcibly the distinctness with which the district is set off from the so-called better parts of the town. People do not decline to go into the

business sections in search of amusement, but they
do hesitate for that purpose to come to the South
End.

The prices at the Columbia are higher than at
the Grand or the Grand Opera, — twenty-five,
fifty, and seventy-five cents. There are eight performances each week, on every evening and on
Wednesday and Saturday afternoons. The variety
features are fewer and they are introduced in appropriate places in the course of the drama. For
instance, in a scene on a levee at New Orleans, a
number of negroes are collected together and quite
naturally begin to sing. The effect is less scattered, but it delays the play, and is hardly so
satisfactory to those who enjoy the variety. The
kind of play presented does not differ materially
from that of the Grand or the Opera, — unless
possibly the Columbia inclines a little more to the
sensational in which there is a good deal of shooting and where the playwright for a grand finale
massacres most of his characters. Irish comedy is
a strong feature of the house. Andrew Mack in
" Myles Aroon," William Barry in " The Rising
Generation," and Joseph Hart in " A Gay Old
Boy " are samples of bills in the comic vein. As
would be expected, plays by better known writers, and also the more recent plays, are given.

" A Trip to Chinatown," " On the Mississippi,"
" Down in Dixie," " The Rainmakers," " The Great
Northwest," " The Great Train Robbery," " Girl
Wanted," and " Boy Wanted " have been among
the attractions of the past year. There is a noticeable unevenness in the character of the programme presented at this house. Sometimes the
bill offered compares favorably with those of downtown theatres; again it approaches the level of
the Grand or the Opera. The management seems
hardly to have decided definitely to compete for
the South End patronage exclusively. Accordingly it oscillates a good deal, and hence the variation just referred to. There is usually a change
of programme each week. The present lessees
conduct theatres in Brooklyn, Pittsburg, and Philadelphia; and they have a considerable number of
traveling companies under their control.

The capacity of the house is sixteen hundred.
The management claim an attendance of ten thousand a week for their eight performances. The
gallery with its twenty-five cent seats represents
the highest price paid for amusement by the great
proportion of the people of the district. There is
local recognition of a distinct gradation in rank
from the Grand through the Opera up to the
Columbia. The Grand and the Opera are the

usual places; the Columbia is an extravagance to be enjoyed only on rare occasions.

During the past year, and especially since the Grand Opera House has returned to its former efforts to maintain a high-priced theatre in the South End, there have been a number of indications that the Columbia in turn may change in the opposite direction, — giving up its former policy of catering to the wider theatre-going public of the city, and inclining more and more to look for its support to the people of the district. "Cut-rate matinees" have been announced, at which prices have been specially reduced. Not long ago a season of light opera with prices as low as ten cents was advertised.

These three theatres comprise the really popular amusement resorts of the South End, places which are intended primarily for and which minister chiefly to this part of the city. The entertainment offered, while very frequently coarse, is yet rarely immoral or suggestive. Omitting the vulgarity of much of the humor, it may truthfully be declared that a large part of the amusement tends to awaken good emotion among the patrons. Bravery, loyalty, faithfulness, and honesty are virtues frequently portrayed, and always applauded by the audiences. Much more can be said in favor of

the moral influence of the local melodrama than of
many of the productions of our so-called first-class
theatres.  In general, objectionable features are
much more likely to be found in the higher-priced
theatres than in those which are here described.
There is, however, a cheap theatre just beyond
the inner limits of the district which panders to the
demand for the suggestive or the immoral.  The
bills teem with features which are just within
the bounds of decency required by law; not infrequently, too, it transgresses even such limitation.  From its location so near the South End,
it undoubtedly draws very largely for its support
upon the people of this district.  But its habitués
are by no means confined to the South End.  Its
patrons come from all parts and from all classes of
the people; for the depraved and vicious instincts
to which it ministers are not the exclusive possession of the unprivileged.

Of quite a different character from the places of
amusement that have been passed in review is the
Castle Square Theatre, which was opened in 1894,
for the production of plays by a stock company.
This venture not proving successful, a change was
made to a " combination " house ; and successive
companies presented a variety of bills of the usual
character.  The second venture likewise proving

unsuccessful, the manager was told to try a scheme of his own ; that of an opera house, producing light and grand opera at popular prices. In the spring of 1895 the experiment was initiated, first with " The Beggar Student " and then with " The Bohemian Girl." The latter was a great success from the beginning. Crowded houses and ample financial support gave a complete indorsement to the undertaking, and exceptional interest was taken in it because of its novelty.

The stock company consisted of about fifty members, eight or ten of whom were capable of the leading parts. The remainder took minor parts and formed the chorus. As a rule an opera was given for a week at a time. Among the operas presented were " The Mikado," " Maritana," " Faust," " Rip Van Winkle," " The Huguenots," " Carmen," " Aida," " Martha," " The Chimes of Normandy," " The Pirates of Penzance," " Fra Diavolo," " Pinafore," " Cavalleria Rusticana," " Il Trovatore," and " Olivette." Grand opera was the more popular, probably because it had never before been given at popular prices in Boston. Light operas were used chiefly to ease up the company from the heavy strain of continued work in grand opera. As the success of the enterprise became more certain, the plan was adopted of having two singers alternate in the presentation of a single part. The company was thus enabled to do better work. The cast was gradually strengthened by the engagement of superior artists, and the repertoire was also increased and improved. Rehearsals were constantly kept up of new operas to be presented and old ones to be revived. Popular operas such as " Carmen," " Faust," " The Mikado," " The Bohemian Girl," and " The Chimes of Normandy," were repeated at more or less regular intervals.

Much of the success of this operatic experiment was due to the ability of the original manager. With wide theatrical experience, he was prepared to cope with the difficulties of the undertaking. He possessed a further advantage above ordinary managers of popular theatres, in that he did not approach the experiment solely from the point of view of financial profit. His first care was for an artistic success; and he was also deeply interested in the undertaking as an effort to give a good performance of opera at prices within the means of the people. He was confident, however, that money would be made in the end; and the experience of the Castle Square has justified his prediction. After the success of the experiment had become assured, he retired from the management.

The patronage of the Castle Square was of course not limited to the South End. Its popular prices at all times, and its charge of twenty-five cents for admission to all parts of the house on Monday evenings and Wednesday afternoons, brought it within the means of all except the very poor. Still it must be remembered that even such a price presents difficulties to the majority of the people of such a district as ours. The larger portion of the patrons were drawn from a much wider circle, from the city in general and from the suburbs.

Musical taste also had much to do with the character of the audiences. Love of really good music does not yet exist to any great extent among local people. Their demands are fairly well satisfied by the street pianos, the band concerts, and the efforts of the poorly trained singer and musician such as are found in the cheapest amusement places. The possible influence of such music as was regularly given at the Castle Square, could its influence be brought to bear generally upon the people of the South End, cannot be easily overestimated. The chief criticism of the Castle Square which must be made from the point of view of this study, is that somehow it did not find a way of reaching the people in its immediate vicinity — a

great working-class population which needs it so
much more than do the residents of more favored
sections.

After two years of great success as a popular
opera house, the Castle Square underwent a complete change. For the summer months of 1897, a
stock company for the production of standard and
new plays at popular prices was announced. The
summer season proved so successful that the new
policy was continued in the autumn, and apparently the theatre has permanently departed from
its former plan.

The change is to be regretted by all lovers of
music, and especially by those who are interested
in the educational influence of such music as was
furnished by the Castle Square. At the same
time the new plan is interesting as an experiment
in popular amusement. Standard and new plays
of a high order are given at lower prices than have
ever before been known in Boston, for such a
quality of entertainment. Two performances take
place daily. Amusement of the best character is
thus provided for the people of the South End in
one of the most beautiful theatres in the city, at
charges within the means of most working people.

The Hollis Street Theatre is located within the
limits of the district, but it has no more relation to

its surroundings than the Drury Lane in London. It is perhaps the highest grade theatre in Boston.

Next in importance to the theatres as amusement resorts are the numerous public halls scattered through the district, but to be found in greatest number along Washington Street. In these halls different groups of people gather more or less regularly throughout the year. Clubs, trade unions, and other organizations occupy the halls very frequently in a round of annual balls. Dancing classes and the socials connected with them form a conspicuous part of what goes on in these halls. Each popular teacher has his or her headquarters where classes are formed, and where special instruction is provided for past and present pupils and their friends. These affairs must not be confounded with the low forms of amusement to be found in the sailors' dance halls of the North End. A few halls in our district, regularly given over to dancing, have a bad reputation. The dancing classes and occasional balls, however, are patronized mainly by respectable working people. Admission is charged for both men and women, and the proprieties of social intercourse are fairly well observed. These assemblies are composed chiefly of young men and young women employed during the day, who after their work crave some free and unconventional recreation. Though the dancing and the music are rarely good, and signs are not wanting of the influence of the stage upon some of the dancing, there is little that is seriously objectionable although there is much that might be improved.

Beside the theatres and the social life which centres in the halls, there is a variety of minor amusements.

The Aquarium, which has recently ended its career of a twelvemonth, was the most pretentious of these smaller places. To give color to its name there were a few glass tanks of fishes. There was varied entertainment of a poor sort in the way of singing, dancing, sleight of hand, and athletics. A stage show was given at intervals. There was a general ten-cent admission, with additional fees of five or ten cents for special exhibitions. On Shawmut Avenue near its junction with Tremont Street, is a small theatre of a still meaner type, known as the Royal. After the completion of a programme of songs and dances of a vulgar and commonplace character, the audience is invited to adjourn downstairs, where are arrayed a few articles of curiosity, — snakes, fishes, or some stuffed animals. In connection with the other attractions of the Royal, there is also a shooting-gallery.

From time to time exhibitions of a similar catch-penny character appear in vacant stores along Washington Street and remain for varying periods of a few weeks or a few months. There is an out-of-doors shooting-gallery on Washington Street, open except in the coldest weather, where for five cents one can have shots at the most hideous look-ing figures imaginable. This gallery furnishes one of the favorite trifling interests of the district. Now and then a merry-go-round, with its accom-panying attractions, establishes itself on a vacant lot on Albany Street near Dover, and during a few weeks gathers for its owners a goodly harvest of pennies and nickels. Not long ago such a show stationed on this lot had among its attractions aerial swings, an "Eden Musée of Wax Works and Fine Arts," a "Barnum's What is It," and a shooting-gallery. In the evening the scene was really picturesque and interesting. There was the noise of discordant music, the glare of the elec-tric lights, and the gaudy decorations of tents and booths, — all in the midst of a dimly lit, squalid neighborhood. The seats and the swings were crowded with eager amusement-seekers. Located in the midst of the tenements, the show drew not only the usual crowd of men and boys, but all the women of the families, young and old.

Scattered through the district are many billiard and pool rooms and a number of bowling alleys. The saloons, while giving opportunity for a certain sort of social intercourse, can hardly be said to provide any real recreation. These complete the list of all organized South End amusements which are the natural outgrowth of the needs of the inhabitants. This list furnishes the local illustration of what private enterprise, having in mind the making of money, provides working people for their relaxation and refreshment.

The sights and sounds of the street constitute an important part of the recreative resources of the district. Their hold upon the people is well seen by the sense of desolation which tenement children feel when they go to the country ; or by the hesitancy shown by their elders as to removing to the suburbs. The patrol wagon, the fire engine, the ambulance, the general passing show, and even the rows of shops, enliven the monotony of an existence in which wholesome amusement is sadly lacking.

Family and neighborhood life contribute their share of entertainment and variety. Births and deaths, weddings and funerals, are made to satisfy the demand for excitement and for the exercise of the powers of the imagination. The wake still occasionally takes the form of a melancholy pleasure among the Irish population. From time to time their generous impulses lead them to arrange raffles and balls for the benefit of some unfortunate neighbor. On any informal social occasion, there are always those present who can "do a turn," to the pleasure and pride of their friends. The children have their festivals, — confirmation in church, graduation from the grammar school, and some sort of distinguishing mark given to the day on Christmas and the Fourth of July. Up to the limits set by the street and the policeman's presence — often the limits are too narrow — youthful spirits contrive the same range of sport and mischief as they do under easier conditions elsewhere. The happiness that belongs to the inner life of the family is cultivated much more by the Jews than by the Irish; but the Irish, with their constant flow of humor, can develop in some narrow back street much of the social give and take, and many of the friendly amenities that are characteristic of a country village.[1] From this general point of view there is a pathos about lodging-house existence such as the tenement house, with home and neighbors, does not even suggest.

[1] See the chapter on "A Tenement Street" in Mr. Sanborn's *Moody's Lodging House.*

The large amount of work for social improvement done in our district has one of its best results in the way of developing a happier home and neighborhood life. It is also true that the picture shows, concerts, and courses of entertainments, which are given in connection with college settlements, working people's institutes, and churches, illustrate the possibility of a gradual improvement in amusements. The constituency of these is in each case limited, however, because they are associated with other interests and in some cases have ulterior motives. The real need is for some large public resort which shall furnish amusement at once uplifting and adapted to popular needs.

We may easily exaggerate the amount of harm that results from the ordinary amusements of such a district as the South End. The important point is not the harm done, but the good left undone. The hold of the theatre upon the masses of the people constitutes it one of the greatest educational fields. Of the principal local theatres, one distinctly abuses this opportunity; one takes hold of it in a commendable way; the others in general simply let it slip.

# CHAPTER IX

## THE CHURCH AND THE PEOPLE

THE district covered by the present investigation is provided with a good number of organized religious agencies. There are in its half a square mile of territory twenty-two churches, — three being Roman Catholic, seventeen Protestant of various denominations, and two Jewish synagogues, — besides four rescue missions, two corps of the Salvation Army, and one corps of the Volunteers of America. It might seem, therefore, as though the spiritual needs of every nationality, class, and type would be adequately met.

The Roman Catholic churches easily come first in size and importance. One of them is German, and many of its parishioners live in Roxbury. The two others, one the Cathedral of the archdiocese, together with a fourth on the outskirts of the district, shepherd practically the entire Irish population. A French Catholic church, a little distance away, cares for people of that nationality throughout the city.

Like most Roman Catholic churches, each of these includes within its organization sodalities for religious instruction and the promotion of a stricter observance of the sacraments; a Society of the Sacred Heart, whose aim is to foster a devotional spirit; temperance societies for young men; and a conference of the Society of St. Vincent de Paul, the great charitable organization of the church.

Besides the usual varied religious services, all five hold parochial missions once or twice a year. These in purpose and method closely resemble revival meetings and protracted services. One would often find the exhortation much the same as he might hear from a conservative Protestant pulpit. The aim of the missions is "to rouse the careless and indifferent, and to excite increased earnestness and devotion on the part of those who make a profession of religion." A mission lasts usually two weeks, one week for men and one week for women. While it continues, the church is thronged every evening, people leaving their work and their amusements to attend; and a noticeable seriousness comes over the entire Catholic population. At such times, and more or less throughout the year, workingmen with their dinner pails may be seen coming and going from the churches in the early morning hours.

The activity of the Catholic church centres, of course, in the clergy. First and above all, they conduct the large number of formal religious services on Sunday and during the week, which go with their system. They arrange for such special services as have just been mentioned, — the actual conduct of these services being usually in the hands of the priests of a separate evangelistic order. In the next place, the parochial clergy each have their share of confessional duty. Then they have the responsibility of the different organizations within the church. Lastly there is the simple but never-ending round of parochial duties, — sick calls, ministration to the dying, and prayers over the dead. Each church has, of course, a considerable clerical staff; but when it is considered that the Catholics of this district number about two fifths of the population, it will easily appear that the priests are very hard-worked men.

It seems to be repugnant to Catholic theory that the church should enter into the non-religious life of its adherents, aside from its traditional work of education and charity. The Cathedral exemplifies this theory more fully than the other churches, partly because it is involved in so many of the wider interests centring in the duties of the archbishop. St. James' Church is well organized for

parish work, and carries the loyalty of its people
to an unusual degree. The young men are drawn
into the great double choir, which is under one of
the ablest and most popular musical conductors in
Boston. The choir gives occasional public recitals.
The young men's sodalities have social as well as
religious features in connection with many of their
meetings; now and then throughout the year various other organizations within the church have
gatherings for the sake of recreation and friendly
acquaintance. The German church has a parish
house, one of whose uses is that of social headquarters for the parishioners. A bar in the principal hall supplies beer and light wines, and is an
important source of income to the church. There
is a flourishing parochial school in this building.
There are small parochial schools for the younger
children at the Irish churches, but attendance
upon them is never insisted upon. As a rule,
the children of Catholic parents attend the public
schools.

Of the two Jewish synagogues in the district,
one is reformed, and draws its large and well-to-do
congregation almost wholly from other sections of
the city. The Jewish population of the district is
predominantly Russian, and consequently of the
orthodox faith. Connected with the orthodox

synagogue is a week-day school of more than one hundred Jewish children for the study of the Talmud, the boys and girls attending on different days. Besides the larger synagogues there are two smaller places of worship, in one of which a daily service is maintained. These smaller places are the headquarters of Jewish societies which combine the functions of public worship with those of a benefit club for sickness and death. Other Jewish associations hold religious services either in their own rooms or in halls hired for the purpose on the Jewish new year and the Passover, if not oftener. A local rabbi claims that comparatively few Jewish families in this district fail to attend public worship at least occasionally. Their religious duties are much interfered with, however, by the increasing custom of working on Saturdays.

Of the seventeen Protestant churches and chapels, five belong to the Congregationalists, two to the Episcopalians, two to the Methodists, three to the Baptists, two to the Presbyterians, and one each to the Lutherans, the Universalists, and the Unitarians. None of them has well-defined parish bounds. Indeed, the intermixture of large foreign elements throughout the district would make distinct parishes impossible. Each of them gleans wherever it can throughout the whole region.

Some of these churches and chapels, on account of changes in the population, have practically lost their hold in their respective neighborhoods, and can no longer be counted as religious factors in the South End. One of the chapels, for instance, which was formerly the seat of considerable aggressive religious work, now keeps up only a small Sunday-school, which includes among its members Jews and Syrians. Quite recently, however, this chapel has become the headquarters of religious and social work among the Armenians. A Baptist church near by, although it has a few attendants living in the vicinity, draws most of its rapidly diminishing audiences from greater and greater distances. Of the congregation of a German Lutheran church which has recently removed, not one resided within the limits of old Boston. The Norwegian and Swedish Lutheran bodies are also widely scattered. These, together with the Swedish Methodist and Presbyterian bodies, are churches rather of a class than of a locality, and need receive merely a passing mention in a study of the religious situation in the district.

The really effective local work of the Protestant religious agencies is being done by five churches ; and, even at that, four of them are situated on the confines of the district under review and have

their chief range of activity without it.[1] These
five fall into two groups: those that preserve the
tradition of the old-time family church, and those
which have departed from that tradition more or
less in order to meet present conditions in the
South End.

To the first group belong the Shawmut Congregational Church and the Clarendon Street
Baptist Church. Both are churches of the well-
to-do middle class. The former has yielded to
the "compulsion of a changed environment" to the
extent of a popular Sunday afternoon or evening service; a reading-room open every week-day
evening; and a young men's social and debating
club, meeting fortnightly. Its actual membership
is about four hundred, and that of its Sunday-
school about three hundred. A small Norwegian
Congregational body meets in its vestry Sunday
afternoons. This church owns the property of
Shawmut Chapel, in the tenement-house section
of the district, where it carries on a Sunday-school.
Preaching services at the chapel are maintained
by the Congregational City Missionary Society.

The Clarendon Street Baptist Church, whose
membership nearly reaches the twelve hundred
mark, has changed but little in the direction of a
wider ministry. A boys' brigade, a singing class

[1] The Church of the Good Shepherd also affects it somewhat.

open to all, and parish relief, constitute the social
phases of a work distinctively evangelistic. The
reason of its strict adherence to what it calls
" straight gospel work" lies in its profound conviction of the nearness of Christ's second coming.
The Gordon Missionary Training School, —
named in memory of its founder, a former pastor
of the church, — prepares young men and women
for Christian service at home and abroad. As a
means of training, members of the school carry
on a systematic house to house visitation for religious conversation and prayer throughout the
neighborhood of the church; they visit wharves
and cheap lodging houses to hold meetings ; assist
in rescue missions ; and carry tracts and flowers to
the sick in hospitals.

The churches that have broken away from the
tradition of the family church and are specially
endeavoring to meet the altered situation in this
section of the South End are Berkeley Temple,
the Every-Day Church, and St. Stephen's. Each
represents a different denomination, — Berkeley
Temple, the Congregational ; the Every - Day
Church, the Universalist ; St. Stephen's, the
Episcopal. The first two reach more especially
the unattached boarding-house and lodging-house
class; the last, the families of working people.

All three specially cultivate friendly relations among their adherents, and aim to minister to man's social and mental as well as spiritual needs.

Berkeley Temple was the pioneer in this direction, and is the largest and most widely known Congregational church in New England. One of the most interesting features is the Temperance Guild, carried on by reformed men, through whose agency large numbers have been redeemed from drinking habits. The Temple, as a part of its reform programme, has been the means of closing many disorderly houses and preventing the opening of several liquor saloons in the neighborhood. An organization called the Dorcastry is devoted to the interests of working women and girls. There are classes in grammar, German, dressmaking, gymnastics, china and oil painting, and other educational and industrial branches. In these various classes, most of which are open to young men also, more than two hundred pupils are enrolled. The Berkeley Temple School of Applied Christianity fits young men and women for the various fields of lay activity. By being detailed to regular duties at the church, the students in this school acquire practical training in Christian service.

Berkeley Temple, of course, puts its great em-

phasis on the spiritual side of life.  Indeed, the
social, educational, and relief-giving phases of its
work are valued chiefly as points of approach to
the spiritual nature.  Taking as its motto, " To
minister in the name of Christ so as to bring men
to Christ," it regards reading-rooms, entertainments, employment bureau, and classes as means
by which man may be brought within hearing of
its message.

Nine religious meetings of various kinds are
held in the Temple every Sunday, beginning with
the prayer meeting of the Brotherhood of Andrew
and Philip in the morning, and ending with an
after meeting for inquirers at the close of the
evening service.  During the week there are seven
prayer meetings of one kind or another.  All these
services are patterned after the ordinary type,
except the Sunday evening service, which is varied
in character, a stereopticon lecture often taking
the place of a sermon.  At a fair estimate fifteen
hundred different men, women, and children, representing fourteen nationalities, pass through the
Temple's doors every Sunday.

It is interesting to note that the Berkeley Temple of to-day is the legitimate outcome of the
original purpose of Berkeley Street Church, whose
successor it is.  When the present edifice was ded-

icated in 1860, the pastor of the church said that the design was to provide the genial home of a missionary church; and a missionary church in the deepest sense, going out to meet men at so many points of need, the Berkeley Street Church has become in Berkeley Temple.

Among the features of the work prosecuted by the Every-Day Church are a reading and recreation room with a lunch counter in one corner, where coffee, sandwiches and cakes may be had at moderate prices; a kindergarten, a day nursery, a stamp savings bank, classes in music, sewing, and cooking; a fruit and flower mission in the summer and fall; entertainments, University Extension lectures, and a social science conference. A small fee is charged for the nursery, the entertainments, and lectures, and for the use of the pool table. Everything else is free. Relief is extended to the poor, and a lawyer may be consulted free of charge by those unable to pay.

Like Berkeley Temple, the Every-Day Church aims chiefly to be an evangelistic agency. In its final influence it would bring men into a Christian life. Failing in this, it would believe that it was not fulfilling its real mission. One of its religious services is a Pleasant Sunday Afternoon, consisting of music, readings, and a brief address, often by a layman.   A daily half-hour service, designed to be simple, quiet, and restful, was maintained for a considerable time, with an attendance ranging from three or four to twenty-five.

St. Stephen's runs a wider range of the social gamut in its constituency than Berkeley Temple or the Every-Day Church.   Aside from the great Roman Catholic centres, it is the one church with an existence of its own that is situated in the midst of the district mapped out and actually wrestles with this district's distinctive problems. While its chosen field is the laboring classes, it includes in its parish not a few residents of the Back Bay.   Rich and poor meet at its services to engage in a common worship, presenting one of the most Christian sights to be found in the city.   It has over five hundred communicants, and about one thousand souls under its care.   Ecclesiastically it is distinctly high church, but not ritualistic.

Among the guilds of St. Stephen's are the Brotherhood of St. Andrew; St. Mary's Ward, a branch of the Girls' Friendly Society; and the Guild of St. Elizabeth for women, especially mothers.   A children's laundry, where little girls are taught to wash and iron, and a kindergarten, are other phases of its work.   The two missionaries have on their visiting list about two hundred families of the poor. A new and well-equipped parish building, called St. Stephen's House, adjoins the church, where also the clergy and several lay helpers reside.

St. Stephen's differs from Berkeley Temple and the Every - Day Church in that it comes at its social work from the religious side. While they would meet men first of all at some point of physical, social, or mental need, St. Stephen's would begin at some point of spiritual need. In Berkeley Temple and the Every-Day Church, reading-rooms, classes, and temporal relief prepare the way for ministry in religious things; at St. Stephen's they follow naturally from religious ministry.

St. Stephen's Rescue Mission for men is an important adjunct of the church. Meetings are held every evening in the mission rooms, around the corner from the church; and a wood and coal yard provides work whereby men trying to reform can earn lodging and meals. A lodging house where a night's lodging can be had for fifteen cents is connected with the mission. Attendance at the meetings varies from seventy-five to one hundred, and during 1897 over fifteen hundred men expressed a desire to live a Christian life. This mission is now the New England headquarters of the Church Army, an organization on lines somewhat similar to those of the Salvation Army, without its sensational and noisy side.

The two most unique religious organizations in the South End are Morgan Chapel and Barnard Memorial.

When in 1869 the Church of the Disciples, of which the Rev. James Freeman Clarke was pastor, removed to its present house of worship, their former church building was purchased by the Rev. Henry Morgan, an independent Methodist minister, for his mission then carried on in a neighboring schoolhouse. At his death, Mr. Morgan left this property to the Benevolent Fraternity of Churches, a Unitarian organization, with the proviso that the work should be carried on by the Methodists. In the case of Morgan Chapel, therefore, there is the curious combination of Unitarian ownership and Methodist management.

Morgan Chapel unites evangelistic, recreative, educational, and industrial features. It has a variety of religious services, with occasional revival seasons, and even conducts " cottage meetings " in the homes of some of its people, — all of which are infused with characteristic Methodist fervor. Active temperance work goes on. As a means of keeping men's weekly wages from going to the saloons, there is a Saturday evening concert, followed by a social gathering or a temperance meeting lasting until eleven o'clock. The chapel has a considerable following of the very needy. It supplies them with temporary work, and after that, so far as possible, regular occupation is found for them.

Barnard Memorial, formerly Warren Street Chapel, is probably not duplicated anywhere in its special function of "a church for children." It was founded by the Rev. Charles F. Barnard in 1836. The history of the chapel is one of much interest. Since 1832 Mr. Barnard had been gathering about him the children of the neighborhood, — at first in the parlor of Miss Dorothea Dix, afterward in the Hollis Street Church, and later in the old school building on Common Street. The picture before his mind and governing his activities was that of a religion for children neglected by parents and churches, and of an attractive place where the services on Sunday and the instruction and amusements on week-days would be suited to a child's need.

Barnard Memorial is still conducted upon the lines laid down by its founder. A preaching service for children and a Sunday-school are held each Sunday. A free day school opens its doors to all children who through physical or mental disability cannot attend the public schools. There is a sloyd class, a kindergarten, and an evening school, all sustained by the City. The week's programme is well filled with club meetings designed to furnish instruction and entertainment.

The religious side of the work of the chapel is still held to be of primary importance, — the other phases of it being regarded as means of attracting children into Sunday-school and church. The members of the various clubs and classes, with the exception of those maintained by the City, are drawn mainly from the regular Sunday attendants.

However, since Barnard Memorial was started sixty years ago, the situation in the neighborhood has radically changed. Few if any of its old families are left, and the places of those who have moved away have been taken largely by foreigners. Moreover, the chapel was practically the sole possessor of the field in 1836 ; but there are now nine other Protestant churches in its old territory. As a result of this changed situation, the sale of the chapel with a view to rebuilding elsewhere has been contemplated. If this sale were made there would be another building in the South End which, having served its religious purpose, had been handed over to other uses. To this group belong already the Hollis Street Theatre, once the Hollis Street Church; the Columbia Theatre, into which is incorporated the church where Dr. Edward Everett Hale began his Boston ministry, becoming later, under the name of the pro-cathedral, a Roman Catholic church, remaining so until the present Cathedral was built; and the building on the corner of Washington and Pine Streets, — which houses the Salvation Army, but has had the now defunct Aquarium for its chief feature, — formerly the Pine Street Church, where Professor Austin Phelps was pastor for some years.

The various rescue missions, the Salvation Army and the Volunteers of America, dealing as they do chiefly with the roving class, affect but little the permanent religious situation. Thousands of men drift into these missions during the year. The Salvation Army deals with the casual and semi-criminal classes more directly, perhaps, than any other religious organization. Six slum sisters live in some of the meanest streets, in order to help fallen women. At the Army headquarters a Workingman's Hotel has been opened, where men are lodged at prices ranging from five to fifteen cents. In connection with this lodging house there is a wood yard. The familiar street-corner meetings are courageously carried on through a large part of the year. Though the Salvation Army lass receives the same consideration and sympathy here that is given her in every such quarter, the " war " in this district is unfortunately not very successful. The meetings at headquarters seem to be attended mainly by members of the Army and their direct beneficiaries.

There are two centres of Christian influence among the Chinese, in addition to the special provision made for them by two or three churches in the way of Sunday-school classes. One is a Chinese Young Men's Christian Association, which occupies a small building quite near the Clarendon Street Church. On the ground floor is a laundry; but on the floor above are reading and recreation rooms, and two sleeping-rooms for visiting members. This is the religious and social headquarters of the Christian Chinamen of Boston and vicinity. A service which is open to all is held here each Sunday afternoon. With but thirty-five members, this association is entirely self-supporting. The other effort is a Chinese mission conducted by a native in Chinatown. There is preaching, a Sunday-school, and a Christian Endeavor meeting on Sunday; and classes for the study of English are held one evening a week. As to such work, it is difficult to tell whether it has any religious value. A few Chinamen are members of South End churches.

Morgan Chapel is situated so as to deal with the largest group of colored people. That neighborhood also constitutes part of the responsibility of Hope Chapel, a useful centre sustained by the Old South Church. A colored congregation has recently established itself near the Bradford Street colony.

In a section where so large a part of the population is free from the usual restraint of the home, and is living out of normal relations with its surroundings, many forms of fantastic and materialistic belief might be expected to find adherents. Such phenomena illustrate at once the reality of the religion and the present inadequacy of the church. The followers of these vagaries represent types of people who under ordinary conditions would find satisfaction in some form of Protestant worship. Spiritualism in all its phases has a strong intrenchment throughout the South End. Here are to be found mediums of every kind, — clairvoyants, palmists, astrologers, magnetic and inspirational healers, psychometric readers, and mahatmas. Unquestionably many of these are honest, but not a few use such titles as a method of advertising a degraded calling.

Numerous societies of Spiritualists have their headquarters in our district. The Boston Spiritual Temple, and the Boston Spiritual Lyceum, a Spiritualist Sunday-school, are the most important local organizations of this cult. There are many smaller groups which meet in various halls. All charge a small admission fee to their meetings. A meeting is often opened with singing of gospel hymns and prayer, and closed with the benediction. An address, followed by " tests," is always given. The speaking is often "inspirational." One of the commonest tests is " readings," or " delineations," or " sensing," — three names for the same thing. Various articles are placed upon a table, and as the medium takes them up he endeavors to describe some scene or incident associated with them, or some of the characteristics of their possessor. Any approximation to fact is gladly " recognized." At one place " spirit faces " are developed on photographs brought to the meeting. Cabinet manifestations of any sort are but rarely given. A long array of mediums is on hand to take part in these meetings, which serve them as points of approach to the public. Ten or a dozen of these persons is not an uncommon number at even a small gathering.

The churches and missions that have been enu-

merated and described include by no means all
the religious activity that goes on in the district.
Many other agencies with headquarters elsewhere
carry on work within its borders. Representatives of the different city missionary societies, and
visitors associated with churches in other quarters
of the city, go about among the poor and minister
to their needs of body and spirit. On the other
hand church-going among the people is not confined to churches of this immediate locality, but
extends to those elsewhere in the South End and
in the neighboring sections. It is probable that
the district is represented in nearly every church
and religious society in the city.

What, then, is the religious situation in this
part of the South End?

The Roman Catholic Church is, on the whole,
holding its ground to a remarkable degree. Yet
it meets with loss in two ways. There is a tendency for young men to become indifferent, and
detach themselves altogether. What is more serious than that, however, is the merely superficial
connection which many people keep up with the
church. These things are the result largely of
moral indolence, but in part they represent intellectual doubt and revolt from priestly authority.
To serious minds, still retaining their instinctive

loyalty, the church will gradually, no doubt, adapt itself. For the others, the outlook is rather dark. A more efficient system of Sunday-schools and more thorough pastoral visitation will certainly be necessary. One would be rash to say off-hand that the Catholic churches ought to institute a concrete social campaign. The very aloofness of the clergy from lay interests contributes to that great moral reserve by which the church is able to touch life at a few points of vital need with supernatural power. This it does, not only in the larger ecclesiastical relation, but in the inner privacy of the home as well, by its solemn presence at great crises of the family life. The Roman Catholic church is in some respects the foremost positive agency for good in the district. Its formalism and its unenlightenment, like the characteristic defects of Protestantism, are the reverse aspect of its qualities.

The Jewish element in the population is attached, in a casual way, to the ministrations of the synagogue ; but the necessities of alien conditions, as well as the opportunities, tend to make havoc of Jewish faith. An intense racial loyalty, however, helps to sustain it.

The rest of the population, about half of it in all, scattering and unclassified, is nominally Pro-

testant. A large minority of these are already
quite apart from the church. The Shawmut Congregational Church, situated at one corner of our
district, a few years ago made a religious canvass
covering the territory within a radius of half a
mile from the church, and found that out of the
eighteen hundred Protestant families visited, six
hundred and fifty, or over one third, did not attend
church anywhere. Since then the population of
the region canvassed has changed more or less, but
there is no evidence to show that it has undergone
any considerable change as regards church-going.
Berkeley Temple, also on the edge of our district,
at about the same time took a religious census of
its neighborhood. Of the nineteen thousand individuals, without regard to Protestant leanings, as
to whom it obtained information, four thousand, or
a little more than one fifth, attended no religious
service of any sort. Only a part of each of these
neighborhoods falls within our district, but all
signs point to a larger ratio of non-church-goers to
church-goers within the district than in the localities adjacent to it. It may be said with assurance,
therefore, that in this section of the South End at
least one fourth of the nominal Protestant population has no church affiliation of any kind. Perhaps one third would be a closer estimate, espe-

cially if we should include such as find their way
into the churches only on some special occasion
such as Christmas or Easter.

It is of course difficult to estimate the number
of Protestants in the district who have any habit
of attending church. The five churches and three
chapels that are available will seat only about one
third of them. As the number of those who go
out of the district to church would certainly be
offset by the large number of those who come to
these places of worship from without, we may take
one third as the maximum proportion of Protestant
church-goers. The remaining third is made up of
those who go occasionally, or send their children
to Sunday-school, or merely retain a church connection for appearance' sake.

The Protestant churches are moving toward the
opposite extreme from the Catholic in their atti-
tude toward interests not distinctively religious.
While it is their chief purpose to renew the inner
man, they aim also to impart uplifting influence
directly to the variety of human activities. The
Catholic churches, on the other hand, rely almost
solely upon an overmastering compunction brought
to bear on human nature at its centre. The religious appeal of the Protestant ministers is one of
cheer and a wider outlook. Their preaching is

exceptionally genuine and sincere ; but except at
St. Stephen's, it misses that call to devotion in
which Catholicism, with its vivid sense of the
nearness of God, is so strong. It may be that on
the whole the one type of Christianity counts for
as much with its actual adherents as the other ;
but one has the feeling that something of the
ritualistic, sacrificial system is almost necessary to
express the struggle of life in such a district as
this.

But what of the majority of their natural constituency which the Protestant churches hardly
touch ? The difficulty cannot be that the churches
are not doing sufficient work. All the pastors,
and their associates with them, are diligent, and
too many of them overworked, men and women.
More effort along present lines might result in
somewhat larger audiences and a lengthened membership list, but would not materially change the
situation. The work done is certainly enough in
quantity for different results. Nor can it be said
that the churches have not fully tried the experiment of popular services and entertainments. A
perusal of the church bulletin-boards and the Sunday announcements would convince one that some
churches, at least, are going to extreme lengths in
these directions.

The situation must be explained, if at all, on different grounds. An important reason for the difficulty is that the churches have no parishes. This has already been noted. Because of it the churches do not get at the neighborhood or, in many cases, the family, in its entirety. There is no concentration of effort upon a given locality or social group. This evil is reinforced by the fact that about half the Protestants of the district have neither settled abode nor family tie. Christianity presupposes the family. Home attachments make real the broader and higher relations of morality and religion. It is on account of this lack that there must be churches of the institutional type in lodging-house regions, whose object is to lay some healthy, albeit artificial, social foundation for the higher life; because the natural one does not exist.

The churches do not join hands to encompass the whole situation. Taken together, the Protestant churches do not present a solid, imposing front that impresses the imagination as do the Roman Catholic churches. On the contrary they exist independent of, and almost unknown to, one another. There is very little proselyting among different Protestant denominations, as there is very little between Protestants and Catholics; but, for the lack of some positive common understanding, the churches work at cross purposes, in patches, and uneconomically.

There are many other possible grounds of explanation. A plan is tried for a time and then given up for some newer plan. There is a lack of continuous effort on a few simple, broad lines. Few if any of the churches look carefully after their members, much less after all who attend their services. Almost none have a comprehensive knowledge of their respective neighborhoods. Says Walter Besant: " In a well-worked London parish there is not a house whose character is not known to the clergy." If all the churches, within and without the district, that are responsible for its religious welfare, should combine their knowledge of the district, many individuals, homes, blocks, streets, and sections, would without doubt be unaccounted for.

But would the Protestant churches as at present constituted be able to meet fully this religious situation, if they were raised to their highest point of efficiency? Probably they would not. With greater efficiency in their present lines of work they would achieve more, but still fall far short. The ordinary Protestant church as it is at present can reach men of a certain sort only; it cannot

reach men of all sorts.   If we observe the kinds of
people that the Protestant churches are getting
hold of, we shall see that these kinds are few in
number.   Even a church like Berkeley Temple
with its varied work gets hold of comparatively few
types of men.   According to its pastor, it touches
and brings permanently within its influence not
more than two or three of the strictly non-church-
going class within a  year.

The feeling of a considerable part of the local
community toward the churches is matter for serious concern.   The working people, especially those
in the various  labor  organizations, regard  the
churches with  more or less  indifference, if  not
with actual hatred.   In other words, there is a per-
ceptible  and  constantly  increasing  estrangement
between  the  working  classes, as  such, and  the
churches.   While this may be and undoubtedly is
to a large extent the  fault of the working classes
through their misunderstanding of the real spirit
of the churches, yet to a  greater extent it is the
fault of the churches themselves.   Instead of de-
voting themselves solely to the moral leadership of
the community, the churches are engaged too much
about  dogmatic  creeds, for which  the  ordinary
workingman has no taste.   Very largely, also, their
members represent, perhaps  unwittingly, the atti-

tude of a superior social class both in their informal relations among themselves and in their
dealings with working people. There is no true
democracy either within the church or where the
church comes in contact with the community.
While the Roman Catholic church is free in a
measure from the taint of social distinction, yet,
even there, for a man who has been bred in the
bracing democratic atmosphere of trade unionism,
the Roman Catholic church with its autocratic
system of government becomes difficult, if not impossible. The great trouble with the church is
that the persons who compose it have never yet
come into the right sort of personal human relations with men. Without that the religious message of any time can never be real.

The sum of all the difficulties that beset the
church in both its branches, here as elsewhere, is
the many-sidedness of modern life. The church
is at the turning of the ways. The Roman Catholic branch holds closely to the simplicity of devotion, consenting to give up even its ancient policy
as to the education of the young. The Protestant branch is going out into service among the
confused conditions which challenge it. The Protestant situation is much more serious than the
Catholic, but that is partly because it is further
developed.

In the midst of this doubtful situation there exists one unchangeable and, in the long run, sufficient source of confidence. The power of faith may languish, loyalty to the church may shrink, but there is still in the heart of the people a constant undercurrent of essential religious feeling. Even among those whose lives are evil, one comes after a while to expect certain instant noble impulses. As Canon Barnett of Toynbee Hall has said about the men and women of East London, "Many have given up religion altogether, and carry about a buried life. It is buried, but it is not dead. When it really hears God's voice, it will rise."

# CHAPTER X

THE larger proportion of the children of this district live in the midst of some, if not all, of its evils, — the industrial struggle, intemperance, ugly surroundings, vice, ignorance. The public schools, therefore, have a difficult missionary task to perform. They are called upon, not only to give a certain amount of book-learning, but to bring light and life and social healing. Among the forces at work for the upbuilding of the local community, the public school, at least in scope, stands first. It is the one institution which touches every family. The law requiring the attendance of all children between eight and fourteen years of age, which is faithfully enforced, gives the schools a full harvest of influence with the entire child life of the district. With this reach of power, the schools make the essential beginnings both of individual and collective development.

The school is an important agency for righteousness. It imparts knowledge and the discipline which goes with knowledge. It demands punctuality, order, obedience; it attempts to administer equitable rewards and punishments; and in these ways brings the pupil early within the realm of government. The school presents to the child new standards in the person of its teachers, new moral visions in the great men and women of history.

The local problem of education, which is made serious enough by scant home training, is much complicated by the varied racial character of the population. Returns from four schools situated at different points in the district will sufficiently indicate this. At the Wait School the pupils are divided as follows: Jews, 57 per cent; Irish, 14 per cent; Germans, 4 per cent; other foreigners, 7 per cent; Negroes, 4 per cent; native Americans, 14 per cent. For the Brimmer School, the returns are: Jews, 25 per cent; Irish, 20 per cent; Germans, 3 per cent; other foreigners, 20 per cent; Negroes, 7 per cent; native Americans, 25 per cent. For the Quincy School: Jews, 19 per cent; Irish, 31 per cent; other foreigners, 18 per cent; native Americans, 32 per cent. For the Franklin School: Jews, 18 per cent; Irish, 29 per cent; Germans, 1 per cent; other foreigners, 18 per cent; Negroes, 9 per cent; native Americans, 25 per cent.

In the assimilation of this heterogeneous mass into American unity, the schools certainly are the most potent factor. In the first place, all pupils have equal rights, equal obligations in the school-room. The English language, with its associations and traditions, is the only one taught. American history not only familiarizes children with the political institutions of our country, but is constantly made to appeal to the foreign-born child as it touches the history of the country he has left. The exercises on Friday afternoons and just before holidays, in which selections from the masterpieces of great American statesmen are spoken, and the saluting the flag, as the symbol of a common country, by Jewish, Irish, German, Italian, and American-born children, are effective in stimulating the sentiment of patriotism. The pictures and busts of notable Americans found in the schoolrooms help to give the children a more distinct national feeling. The results accomplished by the local schools in imparting sound patriotic sentiment is obvious and gratifying to any one familiar with their constituency. The interest of the children in the history of the United States is in many cases almost insatiable.

The more general influence of the schools toward assimilating the new generation is equally marked.

Irish children respond to this influence most readily. They show special capacity for entering into the enthusiasm that goes with the city and the nation. Italian children have much of this same adaptability. The work of the schools in this direction has an immediate and substantial effect in bringing about social solidarity. The local community is ploughed through by most of the racial and religious prejudices of European history. The public school is serving as the chief agency for allaying hostility and establishing a basis for new interests and common loyalties.

To the results gained by the schools in instilling intelligence and righteousness where home surroundings are at their worst, and in uniting a confused immigrant population, must be added what they accomplish in the more specific training of child faculty. The diversion of activity and ingenuity from evil ways, and the definite preparation of the child for filling in the largest degree his future place in society, are becoming more and more important motives in elementary education. Their keen significance here can easily be realized by considering some of the effects of the abnormal conditions that exist in this district upon the character of street children. The term "street children" is used advisedly, for as a matter of fact most of the children of this locality live on the street when they are not asleep. The streets educate with fatal precision. Sometimes in a little side street, you will see a hundred children at play. In this promiscuous street life, there is often every sort of license that can evade police authority. Juvenile rowdyism thrives. Disrespect for decency and order is the result. The same thing is revealed by a study of boys' gangs. The jokes, the horse-play, the tendency to ridicule and make light of everything, which are the life of the gang, issue in an essentially lawless disposition. This includes restlessness under restraint, low indulgence, carelessness, oftentimes cruelty. These are the predominating traits in many street children. In some it is so marked that they become "incorrigible truants," or develop criminal tendencies. A small minority of these children manage to keep an obedient, law-abiding spirit, in spite of "street education," although one does not know how. The fact, however, is indisputable that the thing the schools have to contend with, and that which brings shipwreck to much educational effort in the district, is this predominating impulse to get free from restraints. It is easy to see how soon such a quality could develop the lawbreaker. With undisciplined intellectual cleverness or manual deftness it would easily produce the expert criminal.

In two of its methods particularly, the kindergarten and manual training, the school meets the special needs of street children. The kindergarten makes the child a social being. Acts of self-denial, self-control, and courtesy, of regard for the rights of others, and respect for property, teach the child to yield his individual will for the good of the many. Seated in a circle, the interest of each member of the little cosmopolitan group is enlisted in the work of all the others. The kindergarten is a child's democracy, a coöperative state in miniature. The kindergarten also instills a love of the beautiful, and cultivates the taste of children by means of simple but harmonious designs and objects and carefully chosen colors, developing manual dexterity at the same time by the use of these materials. It teaches the child to observe and love nature, to notice natural forms and processes, and to begin to think about the relation of things. By means of its beautiful songs, poems, and stories, it steeps the child's mind in noble thoughts. The whole kindergarten process stimulates reverence, the true spirit of all religion. Such feelings do much to counteract street experiences. Moreover, the kindergarten imparts all its lessons through play. The play world is the real one for children, just as much as the world of work is the real one for men. Here, most of all, can the school supplant the street.

As to actual results, it is a matter of daily observation that there are children constantly coming to kindergartens, uncontrollable at home, — "wooden" children, morbidly sensitive children, aggressively vain children, — who are often rendered tractable and responsive.

It is encouraging that so much of this influence is now brought to bear upon the local district. There are seven public school kindergartens in different neighborhoods, each having from thirty to forty pupils. There might be at least as many more. This is shown by the fact that dotted among the public ones there are four thriving kindergartens under private philanthropic direction.

The kindergarten and manual training are closely related. Manual training is simply the more special and definite. In tenement-house districts manual training is a particularly hopeful form of education, for two or three important reasons. It is practical, because it develops special capacity and often reveals to a boy what he can best do. The majority of boys in such a district as this must turn to some form of manual labor for a livelihood ; and although in many cases there may be no direct connection between manual training and the work undertaken, the dexterity acquired is sure to give greater efficiency. But while this is the most urgent reason, it is not the most important one.

Manual training is corrective and uplifting. If the streets and gang life tend to make boys irresponsible and destructive, then there is specially needed in the tenement-house neighborhoods some interesting creative work. Children left to their natural impulses, provided they have the materials, always turn to making things. Unfortunately, the boys of this locality have few tools and little material with which to make things. Circumstances develop their destructive side. Manual training is a specific; it stimulates the dormant creative impulses, which in turn supplant the destructive tendencies. It is the enemy of indifference and willfulness, because every step requires self-control, thoughtfulness, care. A thing created means for the boy added self-respect. Furthermore, the boy's wood and tools are realities; they register his temper; he must be sincere with them, for his work stands plainly visible, approving or condemning him. All this is not merely theory; five years' experience in manual training with just such boys as have been described verifies every statement made.

Gradually the kindergarten is finding connecting links of hand occupation in the primary schools, which join and reach across to the manual training that has been introduced into the grammar grades. Boys and girls during the three years in the primary school have paper cutting and folding and simple clay modeling, — being a continuation of what they have done in the kindergarten. For the first two grammar-school years the boys have mechanical drawing, and for four years after that, sloyd. The girls after leaving the primary school have instruction in sewing for four years, with one after that in a cooking class. About two hours each week is given to this part of the school curriculum. For some time Boston has possessed a Mechanic Arts High School, which provides more advanced instruction in general handicraft. A few boys from this district are among its pupils.

The manual training scheme in the public school system needs of course to be much enlarged. Some experiments in this direction are being made in the district under private initiative, with the expectation that if they are successful such work will be undertaken by the public schools. These are partly in the way of providing appropriate instruction for boys with artistic sense, and partly of the nature of special trade instruction. It is very important that manual education should not come to an end short of the trade school. This institution Boston lacks. The need of it is apparent. The number of boys who quit school at an early age and are forced to take any odd job that offers, thus growing up to swell the ranks of unskilled laborers, is very large. Some of these boys, the children of recipients of charity, eventually sink into the same class with their parents, and thus without being to blame perpetuate the type of partial dependent. For poor children whose material welfare and moral salvation very largely turn upon getting started in some skilled trade, our system of education is obviously deficient.

So much for the regular school curriculum. Among the teachers of the district there is an increasing feeling that a closer relation should exist between the school and the children's homes. Unfortunately, with over fifty pupils to each teacher it is hardly possible for the schools to undertake further responsibilities. In connection with the kindergartens, where the numbers are smaller, the teachers are on terms of friendly acquaintance with the mothers of the children. At one of the primary schools the parents of newcomers are invited to be present at the school on the opening day, and later in the year the parents of all the children are asked to come at a certain time.

Friendly relations between teacher and pupil in and out of school are very frequent. There is no doubt that most of the public school teachers in the district are conscientious in their work, and desire not only to impart information but to be an inspiration to their pupils. Some show a genuine interest in the welfare of their scholars, and chat with them about home and personal matters, displaying a great deal of tact in doing so. Others do direct charity work among their pupils, or secure the aid of some charitable agency in cases of extreme need. A few from time to time secure places for the parents of some of the children. In reply to inquiries, a small number of teachers report that they have called systematically at the homes of their pupils. Naturally the majority of the teachers find time and strength for their routine duties only. If a boy or girl gives serious trouble, the teacher, instead of calling at the home of the child, usually summons the parent to the school. That there is scant time for visiting in the homes of pupils is true ; but an enlightened discipline certainly requires knowledge of the home and parents of the children. It is to be hoped that ere long definite provision for such effort will be made.

Meanwhile the increase of philanthropic activity in the district has brought into relation with the local schools a number of persons who are acquainted with the homes and families of the children. Occasional valuable conferences are held between groups of school teachers on the one hand and of social workers on the other.

It may be that the growing general interest that is being felt in the schools will bring out volunteer visitors who shall in a more systematic way make the much needed connection between school and home. The interest referred to not only is having an effect upon the general administration of the school system, but is concerned with the sanitary improvement of school-houses and the artistic decoration of class-rooms.

Evening schools are very important educational factors in this section of the city. They provide various grades of instruction for those who for one reason or another have not received an adequate education in the day schools. In other words, the evening school constituency includes every variety of person from the young man who aspires to a college education, but is unable to quit work and go to college, to the poor Russian Jew or Italian who cannot speak English, and is at the mercy of sharpers. The obligation is heavy upon educators, therefore, without being limited by day school methods, to invent attractive ways and means of meeting the complex educational needs of this great mass of defectively educated toilers of all ages, who find little instruction or inspiration in their daily work. There is a special question of justice involved, in so far as the working people have distinct intellectual ability, the value of which is largely lost to themselves and to society on account of their lack of early opportunity. It is necessary to prevent this waste, not only because of the welfare of the uneducated, but also for the patriotic reason that ignorance means weakness and corruption in our democratic system.

That this sort of responsibility is beginning to be keenly felt is shown by the large increase of evening classes and lectures, under public or philanthropic auspices, free or nearly so, in this and neighboring parts of the city. The variety of these is in fact almost bewildering. A list of the various subjects to be treated in a single winter includes eighty-five branches of knowledge. There is certainly no need of more centres for formal instruction. It is important, however, that those who mingle freely among the people should act as propagandists to seek out and stimulate such persons as could profit by the opportunities that are offered.

There are two large elementary evening schools in the district itself, and just beyond its borders is the Evening High School, — all three being part of the public system. The Evening High School is a favorite institution among the wage-earning young men and women of the city. It has a regular attendance during the winter of about 1500. Its standard does not fall much below that of the average secondary school.

Valuable educational service toward meeting the same general need is rendered by some of the philanthropic agencies of the district, — worth the more because it is given a strong setting of neighborhood intercourse and friendly coöperation, — but this will be touched upon in the following chapter.

# CHAPTER XI

## SOCIAL RECOVERY

IT has well been said by Dr. Edward Everett Hale that, so far as he knows, the part of the South End between Dover Street and Pleasant Street is the most " charitied " region in Christendom. The statement might be applied, with but little less force, to the whole of the district under review. Moreover, this result has come about in the space of two decades; though of course there are a few local charitable foundations that go back toward the beginning of the century. The recent and rapid nature of the change in the population of the district is what has called out such unparalleled activity.

Thus far it has been necessary that all the newer social agencies should struggle for individual existence. The only federation that exists in such way as to cover the ground systematically is that of organizations dealing with the problem of material relief. The number and range of the agencies under consideration might suggest a great

deal of confusion and lost force. This evil outcome is avoided to a large extent by the clear distinction of purpose which is usually made. The
policy of intensive effort within fixed neighborhood limits is also quite general. When there is
similarity of aim or when boundary lines overlap,
competition is usually allayed by the prevalent
friendly feeling. This is worth recording; for
Emerson has told us that no one can hate a philanthropist as a philanthropist can.

Much satisfaction might be found in an exhibit
of the particular methods by which ingenious sympathy has touched so many of the people of the
district and brought them under its helpful ministry; but the technique of social effort is a matter
of inferior interest. The supreme question is as to
the actual public worth of all the expenditure of
time, money, and spirit, laid out upon the local
social problem. What effect has it upon great
classes of people? In what degree does it probe
to the causes of social difficulty? Is it rousing
any intrinsic forces, individual and collective, that
may in time become permanent upbuilding factors
in the life of the community?

From the point of view of the merely benevolent mind there can be no satisfactory answer to
these inquiries. It would see the relief office, the

college settlement, and the coöperative bank all engaged in the same endeavor; namely, the doing individual good deeds. Perhaps, however, the mistake of this point of view is sufficiently appreciated by people in general. It is nowadays almost an axiom that unwise charity only increases the burdens of the poor. It will soon be well understood, also, that scattered good impulses of every sort bring forth " vain works " and " deadly doing."

To see truth clearly, however, is not to see it whole. Even the most discriminating relief-giving has no access to the far-reaching causes of poverty; and, if it set itself up as adequate to the problem of the poor, may even accentuate distress. Philanthropic effort, dealing with a wider range of need, may be able to come more closely at causes ; but it is fitful and lacks permanence. There are " philanthropic waves," and often when need is blackest the wave recedes. Sooner or later it will be seen that effort toward social regeneration, like statesmanship, must call out restorative energies which reach as deep as the difficulty and are as lasting in their nature.

Looked at in this way, the agencies for social improvement in the district go into three quite distinct classes. These may be characterized under the analogy of the treatment of sickness. During the acute stage of disease there must be specific remedies of an artificial kind. When this stage is passed there is need, for the time being, of some unusual and specially favoring natural conditions, such as rest or change of scene. Finally, and above all, there must be a radical reorganization of habits, through which the patient, relying upon such means as are continuously accessible to him, shall establish for himself a healthier order of life.

Charity work of all kinds, centring its attention upon the relief of rudimentary human distress as it arises, has from the social point of view a *remedial* effect.

Philanthropic agencies, presupposing the supply of bare bodily wants and providing some of the distinctive means of happy and noble existence, drawing their chief resources from without the life of the district, may be said to serve the valuable *recuperative* function in the cure of social ills.

The really vital policy — within the lines of local action — is the one which aims to build up a better life for the district out of its own material and by means of its own reserve of vitality. In so far as its social undertakings embody this principle, they have the enduring *reconstructive* quality.

The problem of poor-relief throughout the district is divided between the Overseers of the Poor and the Associated Charities. It is understood between the City officials and the private organization that they shall, as far as possible, have separate fields. The Overseers look out for families frequently or chronically in distress, including the half-pauperized, — those whose only gleam of pride in the matter of demanding aid comes from the consideration that some relative has paid taxes, and they therefore are really entitled to a dividend from the City. The Associated Charities take care of those who have not yet made the habit of dependence.[1]

The Overseers, as far as possible, make their clients work for what they receive. Men living at home are required to saw wood for food supplied their families. Homeless men and women are given shelter and food in return for work at the Wayfarers' Lodge and the Women's Shelter, both at the other end of the city. The more extreme

[1] The number of families in the district aided annually by the Overseers averages about five hundred. The number of families in the district which are dealt with each year by the Associated Charities numbers about nine hundred. By a careful estimate, omitting unattached individuals, fully one sixth of the actual families in the district receive some form of material aid during the year. See page 87.

cases of pauperism find their way to the City alms-house on Long Island in Boston Harbor.

Poor people who fall into occasional and temporary distress, and may be kept from becoming chronic charity patients, are dealt with in the more quiet and sympathetic way of the Associated Charities. Three separate committees or " conferences " divide the district among them. The work of each is in the hands of a group of volunteer visitors with a woman agent as paid executive. There are weekly meetings, and the office of each conference is open on certain hours every day but Sunday. In addition to dealing with cases of distress as they arise, the conferences act as a sort of local council charged with the entire charity problem of their respective territories. In the main the visitors come from other parts of the city, but church missionaries and residents of settlements if not members of conferences are at least in constant relations with them. One of the best achievements of the Associated Charities has been in the way of allaying rivalries of different kinds, so far as they affect the relief of the poor.

The Associated Charities supply a registration office and clearing-house, covering, so far as possible, all applicants for alms in the city, and all sources of supply. Technically this organization does not itself give material aid. For this it relies largely upon the old charities of Boston, such as the Provident Association and the Howard Benevolent Society; though of course its own visitors, acting as individuals, often secure what is needed in particular cases.

Many of the wise restraints upon thoughtless giving, to which the Associated Charities for long bore solitary witness, have now been generally adopted throughout the district. Relief-giving by church visitors has taken on this more intelligent character. St. Stephen's Church has a weekly conference of its staff for the consideration of cases of distress. The chapters of the Society of St. Vincent de Paul at the Catholic churches also have meetings every week of their visitors among the poor.

Not unfrequently cases are still found of people who maintain a course of pauperism by systematically securing aid from a variety of sources; but the family records of the Associated Charities, now covering a period of twenty years, more and more effectually prevent this. Begging is comparatively rare in the district. Asking for alms on the streets is forbidden by City ordinance. It is now confined almost wholly to a few pseudomusicians, whose need is often commensurate with their service, and a varying number of men asking at night for the price of a lodging.

The special task of child-saving is in the hands of two societies which, like all the general charities, have their headquarters in the northern part of the city. The Children's Aid Society, a very progressive and efficient organization, devotes itself in a variety of ways to children who are destitute, neglected or wayward, caring both for those remaining at home and for those who are boarded out. The Society for the Prevention of Cruelty to Children takes legal measures for rescuing abused children, whom it ordinarily turns over to the public authorities. The municipal department for the care of children is now in charge of an able unpaid commission, which is fast taking the City's juvenile wards out of institutions and placing them with country families, subject to the constant oversight of the board's visitors.

The day nurseries of the district do excellent child-saving service. Along with the most scrupulous care of the children goes a large amount of visiting in the homes out of which the children come.[1] The nurseries are so distributed as to meet

[1] In all 250 different children are brought to the nurseries in the course of a month, — representing 225 families. A fee of five cents per day is charged.

the full need of the district so far as it concerns
hard-working and deserving mothers who have to
leave their homes during the day. It is a much-
mooted question among nursery workers whether
children both of whose parents are unworthy
ought to be received into the nurseries, lest to do
so should only confirm the parents in their evil
ways. It would seem reasonably clear, however,
that the interest of the innocent and hopeful child
ought to be paramount, and that he should not be
neglected for the sake of gaining leverage upon
his backsliding elders.

Considerable effort is made, here and there, to
provide work for the unemployed. There are
several philanthropic employment bureaus in the
district; and the Industrial Aid Society, which
covers the city in its scope, has frequent appli-
cations from this district. Three local woodyards give employment to about a hundred men at
a time. A temporary home for working women,
without any suggestion of reformatory or even of
preventive purpose, presents to every woman an
escape from the last recourse to which she might
be driven.

The degraded element in the community is not
despaired of, though the results of effort in this
direction are not encouraging. Some interesting

temperance propaganda is carried on by reformed men in public meetings conducted by themselves, and an active temperance campaign goes with the work of the various rescue missions. There is not a little earnest endeavor toward the reclamation of women who lead an evil life. Though the personal devotion shown in this cause is beyond praise, it must be said that there is no form of human helpfulness so totally inadequate to the need it aims to meet. There is, indeed, little ground for hope once the awful step is taken. Such rescue homes as are needed have usually been placed outside of this district, some of them in the suburbs, thus taking their protégées away from the region where their chief temptations lie.

The outline of charitable effort within our boundaries should perhaps include passing reference to several institutions, — the Children's Mission for orphans and waifs, on Tremont Street near the business part of the city; the Working Boys' Home, under Roman Catholic auspices, on Bennet Street; the Boston Female Asylum for destitute girls, opposite the Wells Memorial Institute on Washington Street, the oldest charity in this part of the city; and the Washingtonian Home, an inebriate asylum, on Waltham Street, a relic of the old temperance societies of that name. All of these accomplish useful results, but they have little direct bearing upon the life of the district.

The most searching charity is that which, after relieving acute distress, proceeds to introduce unusual helpful influences in order to ward off the immediate recurrence of the trouble. Such a motive leads at once into those activities which, taken in their relation to social progress, have been described as recuperative. This kind of work has a profound deterrent value; but the great positive use and the absorbing human interest which it has in itself make that consideration merely incidental. The chief reliance in such effort is upon informal friendly acquaintance. This sort of approach, if it be unaffected, has no limits to its efficacy; but naturally it touches first that which is most accessible and most easily influenced, the life of the child. This is the reason why, as philanthropy has developed, the boys' or girls' club has come to be almost as well recognized an institution in the South End as the public school itself.

The two most important centres for boys' and girls' clubs, judging by the quality of the performance as well as by other tests, are the Ellis Memorial Club and Lincoln House. The career of both has been of unusual interest. The Lincoln Club came into existence in 1887 in a very small way, under the initiative of two young women who are still at the head of the enlarged enterprise. The Ellis Memorial Club had a similar and a still earlier origin. The Ellis building contains a gymnasium, ample meeting rooms, and some sleeping quarters for boys who may be temporarily or permanently without a home. It is located at a point about midway between the homes of the club directors, mostly women, in the Back Bay, and the homes of the rank and file of the members, in the South Cove. No club in Boston deals with boys that have more adverse conditions to meet. The close generous relations that exist between the directors and the boys — year after year until boys become men — has been the means of saving a number of the members from an evil course of life before they had entered upon it, or when they had gone but a little way. Some regularly conducted classes are held, and there is a well used library and a small gymnasium ; but the exercises are in the main of a friendly, informal nature. The great object is to secure an influence that will deeply affect the character of the boys. The continued devotion and enthusiasm of the corps of workers, all of whom are volunteers, in a marked way achieves this result. There are now three weekly gatherings, one for girls, one for small boys, and one for youths of sixteen and upwards. During the year there are parties and entertainments to which the families of members come.

At Lincoln House, where in addition to a considerable volunteer force there is a salaried staff, the scheme of club organization is very comprehensive, and there is systematic manual and athletic training. Here, as also at Ellis Memorial, many members of the young men's club have been the boys of the boys' club from year to year in the past. In both cases there is a distinct club spirit, one might almost say a club type. At Lincoln House constant effort is made to relate the club life to the family life of the members and to the positive interests of the local district. There is a degree of sturdy progressiveness about the young men's club. It has hotly contested debates with the Ellis Memorial Club, athletic exhibitions, and dramatic shows. There is nothing in the city so delightful in their way as the dancing parties, given by the young men and women of Lincoln House.

A small organization called the Jefferson Club ought to be mentioned for the interest attaching to its origin as well as for the spirit that has gone into it. This club was founded four years ago by a group of Harvard men, then undergraduates, and has been carried on continuously by Harvard students under leadership transferred from class to class. The Barnard Memorial has always extended its hospitality to this form of work for boys. For long the Lincoln Club met here. Another club under skilled leadership, having now about fifty members, was formed when the Lincoln Club removed to its new building. A unique form of club is that conducted by the Children's Aid Society in various parts of the city under the name "home libraries." There are seven of these in this district. The nucleus of interest is a library of twenty books, — replaced in due season by different ones, — which is kept in some tenement-house home. Once a week some young man or woman, as regular leader, meets the members of each library — usually boys and girls together. The members number eight or ten and live in or near the house in which the books are kept. At the meetings books are exchanged and discussed, and the leader finds a natural means of influence in such conversation and amusements as may follow.

The establishment in this district half a dozen years ago of the two first college settlements in Boston — the South End House, for men, and Denison House, for women — had a distinct influence upon club work for boys and girls. The settlement clubs, as such, do not stand as models of organization; they represent, rather, an important means by which a new moral relation is set up in the ordinary round of neighborhood life. The cardinal points of the settlement policy with regard to the clubs are: that the groups should be small; that the leaders should be "lavish of personal influence;" that, whatever intellectual result may be gained, the really vital thing is to soften and moralize the child in his inner life; that boys and girls should often be brought together in relations of mutual respect and consideration; that the watchword "save the children" is comparatively empty unless that bad home environment is dealt with which so engraves itself upon the soul when it is "wax to receive and marble to retain."

The summer programme of philanthropy in the district is necessarily different from that of the rest of the year. In most cases the interest of club members is held by occasional excursions to the parks or the country. Lincoln House has its own summer cottage, and members of the various clubs all have a visit there, paying a part of their own expenses. A large number of children from the district are sent to the country each summer through the coöperation of local centres with some of the large agencies for that purpose. Of these the "Country Week" committee of the Young Men's Christian Union is the most important. For summer interests regularly sustained within the district each year, there are two sand gardens in schoolhouse yards kept up by the Emergency and Hygiene Association, two summer playrooms provided by the Episcopal City Mission, and a very useful vacation school, chiefly devoted to simple forms of manual training, which is under the direction of Denison House. There is in the district a Flower Mission which sends flowers to hospitals and other institutions. Several branches of "The Mutual Helpers" furnish flowers for the sick and infirm in the tenement houses. The plan is to have bouquets arranged and distributed by members of different girls' clubs that know as neighbors those for whose sake this open country color and fragrance is brought into the city's stifling recesses.

It is curious that more is not done in the district in the way of informal clubs for men. An organization of this kind is just being formed at Lincoln House. Some germs of such a growth may be found in several free reading-rooms. There are now four of these in connection with churches, — at Berkeley Temple, at Morgan Chapel, at Shawmut Church, and at the Every-Day Church. These are of real use, but their value is much restricted, because of being within church walls. There is a different type of reading-room, located in or near a tenement-house neighborhood, from which all taint of improvement is sedulously kept out. Men are allowed to smoke and to wear their hats, if they like, — a measure of thrift as well as of fancy, — and in general are received on their own terms. The first of these was opened by the Ellis Memorial Club. It was in the locality where the club members themselves live, and they gave loyal assistance. Unfortunately it had to be given up after two very successful winters. A similar reading-room, opened a few months later than the original one, is carried on by the South End House. It is by this time an important centre of neighborhood interests among men. The South Bay Club, composed of those who frequent the reading-room, has weekly meetings, lectures and entertainments, and assumes general responsibility for good order at all times. A third reading-room of somewhat the same sort was kept open during the past winter, under the charge of St. Paul's Society of Harvard College. Quite recently a superior kind of reading-room has been opened by Denison House, well adapted to the higher grades of young men in the neighborhood.

The story of well-devised work among women is

a much more satisfactory one. There are several branches of the Association of Working Women's Clubs in this general section of the city. The Shawmut Club is one of the best representatives of these interesting organizations in Boston. It is now in its twelfth year, has its own rooms, and represents a high degree of intelligence and character in its membership. The club has a strong educational bent. The feeling and the habit of independence are studiously inculcated, and the relations existing between the women of leisure who take the lead and the young working women has that wholesomeness which comes of mutual respect and long-continued coöperation.

At all the settlements and at many other centres of influence· special efforts are made to give assistance and encouragement to young women. Increasingly useful and substantial work is also being done for hard-working, overborne mothers, in helping them, both to face their problems and, on occasion, to forget that problems exist. The Women's Club at Denison House is a very successful and progressive organization. At the South End House the women associates conduct a similar club, the good results of which are specially gratifying, because for most of its members the struggle with poverty is an unending one.

It will be noticed that some of the clubs go on by themselves, while the rest revolve about organized centres, along with a variety of other undertakings. As has been shown, the church introduces such work into its programme. Even the politician, in campaign time, stands as patron to a body of impressively named "associates," who have their social headquarters. A number of important agencies include club organization as part of broader schemes. Two of these are large institutes for working people; the others are settlement houses.

The Parker Memorial, situated one block west of Tremont Street, has of late years become a very active institutional agency. It was originally intended to be a Unitarian church, and still has religious services on Sundays. These, and the lectures and discussions on popular topics which occur on week-day evenings, appeal to the rather well-to-do people who live in the immediate neighborhood. The more direct work of the institution, however, touches the large tenement-house population lying a few blocks to the east of the building, and within this district. The constituency of the clubs and classes is largely Jewish, though more children of American parents come here than to other social centres in these parts. The organized work is reinforced by a good deal of visiting among the families represented in the clubs, and by a large amount of informal helpfulness.

The oldest and most important centre of social activity in the South End is the Wells Memorial Institute, for working men and women. Its admirable situation secures the greatest publicity for the advantages in the way of instruction and recreation which it offers. It has not far from two thousand members, most of them scattered through the southern part of the city. The special aim of the classes at the Wells Memorial is to supply mechanics with a higher order of knowledge and skill as to the trades in which they work, and to give to women of the working classes greater facility in the domestic arts. A great deal of attention is given to healthful amusement and friendly intercourse. The atmosphere of the Institute is thoroughly democratic. The members have much of the responsibility in their own hands; and there is a high degree of mutual respect and coöperation between the members and those who have official direction of the Institute. The fact that a large number of trade unions meet in the building, and that the Central Labor Union has its headquarters there, makes the Institute the chief centre of working - class interests in

Boston. It is a specially fortunate aspect of its work that the rental derived from halls and store-rooms in the building, together with the returns from membership and class fees, makes the Institute partly self-sustaining.

At the settlements, club interests represent what is important but not essential. Reliance is placed largely upon simple neighborly relations with people. There are now in the district several groups of persons living together for the sake of combined effort toward social improvement. The first of these was the Andover House, since 1895 called the South End House, which opened its doors in January, 1892. A year later, Denison House was established, under the auspices of the Women's College Settlement Association, a general organization that also maintains settlement houses in New York and Philadelphia. The Dorothea Dix House soon followed. Lincoln House and Hale House are more recent. St. Stephen's House has become a settlement by gradual stages, the force being made up of the clerical and lay staff of the church of that name. Marenholz House, the latest of all, is a residence for kindergartners who coöperate with the South End House. The South End House, Lincoln House, and St. Stephen's House have only men as residents; Denison

House, the Dorothea Dix House, and Marenholz House, only women; Hale House has included both men and women in its resident force.

The Dorothea Dix House is very unassuming and personal in its ways. Its residents have numbered sometimes as many as ten or twelve. They are young women who have regular occupations through the day. An especial interest is taken in children that are in some way associated with the stage. The house was at first on Warrenton Street, and was originally intended to be an adjunct to the Barnard Memorial. It is now located on Chandler Street, a little way beyond the western boundary of the district.

Hale House was at first situated on Decatur Street, but a year ago moved across Washington Street to Garland Street. Its constituency is largely Jewish. It has developed some original and successful methods of organizing and interesting children, and gradually securing the acquaintance and approval of their elders. This settlement has met with some disappointment in securing a regular force of resident workers, but its prospects are at present much more encouraging. Hale House was established by the Tolstoi Club, a group of young men who have met now for nearly ten years under the guidance of Dr. Hale, to whom

every good cause in Boston is debtor. Dr. Hale
has always kept his devotion to his original parish.
Hale House is in the midst of its fast disappearing
relics.

St. Stephen's House is the centre of the St.
Stephen's parish interests. In its admirable new
building, however, there is provision for non-secta-
rian work upon a basis of simple human fellowship
among people of the neighboring streets, most of
whom are Roman Catholics and Jews. Such
breadth of purpose is characteristic of St. Stephen's.

The South End House, Denison House, and Lincoln House represent comparatively long - established and comprehensive plans. The local constituency of all three is mainly Irish. At Lincoln
House the policy of having actual residents is new
and uncertain, but behind its settlement history
proper is a long period of club work done in admirable spirit and with constantly growing effect.
The house has a large force of experienced workers,
and ample resources of every kind. For what it
sets out to do, it is the most successful philanthropic enterprise in the district. In a building
containing varied facilities for its work, there is
now a graded scale of classes and clubs for all
ages and both sexes. The club work is followed

up by acquaintance with the family life, and there are more and more bonds connecting the homes of club members with the house and its workers. Certain territorial bounds are observed. These are too broad to allow of constant acquaintance with the close interlacings of neighborhood interests; but this wider range brings the house into touch with the political and social affairs of an entire ward. The educational opportunities offered by Lincoln House cover a wide range, and are open to outsiders as well as to regular club members.

Denison House is situated in the South Cove, not far from the great wholesale establishments. The streets in its vicinity are inhabited by fairly comfortable working people. The neighborhood in itself is a quiet one, not swept through by great thoroughfares, and sufficiently small in its natural boundaries to allow of thorough acquaintance with its round of life. Two years ago the settlement took a second house, adjoining its original one, and recently some further quarters have been secured. Thus there are now several attractive rooms for social gatherings, together with accommodations for twelve or more residents. Most of the young women, unfortunately, do not remain longer than a single winter; but there is a nucleus of residents who have been at the house for considerable terms, and have developed lines of work that have distinct and positive merit. The informal friendly gatherings for neighborhood people are especially satisfactory. The freedom with which neighbors come to the house is the result of much inside acquaintance with local family life. There are numerous regular gatherings every week. A Shakespearian dramatic company of older boys has met with marked success. During the past year increased results have been gained in the various classes designed especially for working women of very limited early opportunities. A happy thought is embodied in a recent undertaking of Denison House, — a teachers' club, meeting weekly, in which women teachers of all grades, from the kindergarten to the college, come together for friendly intercourse as members of a common craft.

The South End House is at the edge of a neighborhood where unskilled labor and poverty is thickly settled, but it is also close to great streets, crowded corners, glaring shop windows, and theatres with their flaming signs. It has therefore in good measure the opportunity of close neighborhood work, along with constant access to the larger problems of a great working-class district. The resident force number not more than five or six, but an encouraging degree of continuance has been secured, the average stay of all residents up to the present being nearly two years. As at all the settlements, there is a body of associate workers, men and women, to each of whom is assigned some regular duty. The settlement now has three different points of attack upon its neighborhood, — the residence at one end, the club building at the centre, and at the other end the Marenholz House, which assumes the responsibility for all that is done among the smaller children. For neighborhood work it narrows itself to a territory covering not more than ten city blocks, confining its visiting and nearly all of its club privileges to the people living within these limits. There is a variety of informal groups, — most of them for boys and girls, but several for adults. These are not intended to be mainly educational, in the ordinary sense. Their chief result is in the way of establishing personal relations that are the channel of distinct moral influence. The settlement has by this time entered quite deeply into the neighborhood existence ; the more so perhaps because it has developed slowly and has scattered rather than massed its centres of power. In its relation to the general district, the settlement spends a large share of its entire energy in the way of coöperating with

other agencies of all sorts, providing only that the
task to be undertaken is of some positive social
consequence. It has itself taken a leading part in
creating and carrying on two enterprises in which
the people of the district have had a share, — the
South End Free Art Exhibition, which has given
two successful picture shows, and the South End
Musical Union, which for four years has given
an annual series of high-grade concerts, provided
lectures with musical illustrations, and supplied
elementary and advanced musical instruction.

To estimate the value to the district of these
various efforts toward organizing local people for
social improvement is a matter of great difficulty.
It must be remembered that large numerical returns in themselves would mean little. The best
results of such work come only with intimacy ; a
crowd makes that impossible. The fact that most
of the local philanthropic activity takes a very
close range gives a deeper meaning than usual to
such figures as are available.

In the case of the settlements, where influence is so largely personal, this is particularly so.
Denison House and the South End House each
have about 300 people in their neighborhoods coming to them in some regular way. Lincoln House
has about twice that number of regular adherents.

Summing up the returns from all the social centres mentioned, one finds that about 2900 persons from this district are attached to them in some regular way. These represent 1800 families. In other words, seven per cent of the entire population is immediately concerned with these interests ; while upwards of one fourth of the actual number of families [1] are directly or indirectly involved.

For the most part these influences affect homes and neighborhoods as well as individuals. The district is divided into seven distinct neighborhoods. Of the three east of Washington Street — all having tenement population — the first is covered by Denison House, the second [2] by Lincoln House and St. Stephen's House, the third by the South End House. Of the three between Washington and Tremont streets, the one farthest north and the one farthest south are lodging-house quarters, the inhabitants of which are touched as individuals to some extent by churches and general philanthropic institutions in or near the district. The other neighborhood in this strip — in which the population resembles that to the east of it — is

[1] Not allotting the theoretical proportion of families to the lodging-house population.

[2] Two Jewish young women, one a kindergartner, one a student of domestic science, conduct the Louisa Alcott Club in this neighborhood, especially for girls of their own race.

provided for by the Parker Memorial, Hale House, and Lincoln House. There is, finally, the tenement-house neighborhood lying between Tremont Street and Park Square. Parts of this neighborhood, being compactly Protestant, are influenced from the mission chapels in that vicinity, and in one of the streets there is some interesting personal work similar to that of the settlements ; but there is obvious need of reinforcements at this point.

The settlements reach across the line of distinction which, at the beginning of this chapter, was drawn between all sorts of charitable and philanthropic work on the one hand and effort directed toward social reconstruction on the other. It is this thoroughgoing reconstructive motive, taking deep hold upon the district's own organized life, depending largely if not entirely upon its inherent resources, that gives the most solid promise of lasting future results. There is not only a constant tendency for philanthropy to widen its range, — it tends to evolve into something higher. As to the settlements in particular, it cannot be too decisively stated that philanthropy, however well devised, is not their final end and aim. Their real use in the world is to reëstablish on a natural basis those social relations which modern city life has thrown into confusion, and to develop such new form of coöperative and public action as the changed situation may demand. To foster and sustain the home under tenement conditions, to rehabilitate neighborhood life and give it some of that healthy corporate vitality which a well-ordered village has; to undertake objective investigation of local conditions; to aid organized labor both in the way of inculcating higher aims and in the way of supporting its just demands; to furnish a neutral ground where separated classes, rich and poor, professional and industrial, capitalist and wage-earning, may meet each other on the basis of common humanity; to initiate local coöperation for substantial good purposes; to strive for a better type of local politics and to take part in municipal affairs as they affect the district; to secure for the district its full share of all the best fruits of the city's intellectual and moral progress; to lead people throughout the city to join with them in their aim and motive; — this is what the settlements understand to be their vocation; this is the kind of influence which they are silently, year by year, instilling into the inner currents of the district's life.

Much of this kind of influence evades analysis. It comes with every sort of participation in local affairs that is entered into by the settlements. A neighborhood is first permeated with friendly influence. There come to be return currents of confidence that spread from family to family and from street to street. The neighborhood represents a certain industrial stratum. The settlement comes in touch with men and women of that particular class not only in the immediate neighborhood, but throughout the district and throughout the city. In this way there come as a matter of course the beginnings of joint action between residents of settlements and working people for improving the conditions of life and labor among the working classes.

Some tangible results have already been realized. Denison House has for several years continued a series of practical discussions with regard to industrial matters in which employers, students of social questions, and labor leaders have taken part. This settlement has also given much encouragement to women employees of different grades in their efforts toward mutual aid and improvement. Lincoln House has done useful service in encouraging its young men to band themselves together for the sake of reforming some of the worst abuses of ward politics. As against the machine, this movement was not successful; but it gave two hundred voters a taste of political independence which they will not forget. At the South End House, small groups made up of business men and labor men are occasionally brought together for quiet conversation about difficult industrial problems, with the hope that when conflicts threaten there may be on each side certain men who can treat with some of their opponents. Residents of the house are now and then called upon to address trade unions and to arbitrate in case of strike. This settlement has joined with some of the representatives of organized labor in seeking municipal action in the interest of working people. The first hearing before the City Council with regard to a public bath, to be open summer and winter, was called six years ago at the instance of such a group, two of them being residents of the South End House. A resident of the house is now a member of the municipal Bath Commission, the creation of which came about indirectly as a result of that initial effort. The South End House and Denison House have more than once stood by working people in strikes, when their cause was clearly a just one. Representatives of both settlements are associated with a number of trade union members in a " federal labor union," meeting at Denison House, which has for its object to hold organized labor true to its best motives and sustain it in working them out.

Aside from the settlements, the principal form in which philanthropy evolves into social reconstruction is that of economic experiments conducted upon a strictly business basis, touching the housing, the food, or any of the great common interests of the people. The three rows of model tenements in the district shelter about 200 families under thoroughly good conditions at moderate cost, and yield reasonable interest on the capital invested. The Coöperative Building Company, which owns the largest block, now pays an annual dividend of six per cent. There are four self-supporting homes for working girls in or near the district, two under the auspices of the Young Women's Christian Association, one conducted by the Grey Nuns, and one, called Brooke House, associated in a general way with the Working Women's Clubs. These homes shelter 565 women altogether. Preference is usually given to those earning small wages. The average weekly charge is under four dollars. The Young Women's Christian Association also provides a room registry, and maintains the largest employment bureau for women's work in the city.

There are four cheap lodging houses for unemployed men which have a business management moved by humanitarian motives, — the Boston Industrial Home, the Old Comfort Lodging House, and two others, one conducted by St. Stephen's Church and one by the Salvation Army. In these during the winter a total of nearly 400 men are accommodated every night at an average charge of fifteen cents. All except the Old Comfort have woodyards, in which about 150 men find temporary employment. The Industrial Home, by the combination of lodging house with wood and coal business, is a financial success. The other enterprises fall short of this, though they practically pay expenses. The reason why all are not profitable investments is that they are too small and do not have buildings and outfit scientifically adapted to the purpose.

The Boston Bath House Company has also missed complete financial success only because its business has been on a small scale. Its little bath house has, however, done highly commendable service for several years. The opening of the municipal bath house has given this company an honorable discharge.

Four years ago during a time of exceptional stress, some young men associated with one of the settlements undertook to show that a nourishing meal could be furnished for five cents. They were so successful that they were able to turn over their good will to a restaurant company, which has ever since been conducting a paying business on that basis. A very interesting and satisfactory undertaking is that of the New England Kitchen, which sends out properly selected and cooked food at low cost. The object is to have this food serve as an example and set a standard in working-class homes. Under the same management there is also a restaurant which is patronized by working women.

The Stamp Savings Society, which has a number of local stations in this part of the city, represents the first steps in philanthropic banking. The system has the merit of great simplicity, and the use of the colored stamps, indicating amounts deposited, at once arouses the interest of the juvenile depositor. Coöperative benefit societies are numerous among the Jews of the district. Three advanced forms of mutual benefit organization constitute the stout framework of the Wells Memorial. It has two coöperative banks, through which many suburban cottages have been built. The coöperative medical society secures to a family all ordinary treatment by a skilled physician at the rate of five dollars per year. A coöperative list of prices for clothing and all sorts of household supplies is available to all members of the Institute.

The possibility of distributive coöperation has often been canvassed, but it is felt that under the shadow of the great city establishments every small coöperative enterprise would quickly be crushed by overpowering competition. That the coöperative idea is not without its followers is shown by the fact that some of the employees in one of the large piano factories have a coöperative society, with office hours at noon, through which they purchase their supplies.

Independent organization for purposes of recreation, friendly intercourse, and mutual improvement, is in a very undeveloped stage in this district. There are numerous sporadic social clubs, which evolve out of street gangs in the manner explained in a previous chapter.[1] These are very ephemeral, and this is, on the whole, fortunate. They, however, serve to give their members some experience in self-government, and doubtless in due time this form of organization will become more wholesome and consequently more permanent.

The German colony have among them, in addition to the parish house of their church, a well-

[1] See page 119.

equipped gymnasium, or "Turn Halle," which, with the exception of the one at Lincoln House, is the only gymnasium worthy the name within the bounds of this entire district.

The various secret fraternities find some following among the Protestant part of the population. The Odd Fellows, the United Workmen, and the Knights of Honor have headquarters on the boundaries of the district. The Good Templars seem to have more members living in this locality than those societies. Among the Roman Catholics there are a few organizations of this kind, but without vows of secrecy. The Ancient Order of Hibernians exists in some force. All such groups seem unable to rise very high in their morale. About the best that can be said for them is that they offer the deterrent influence of a harmless social centre. Some of them furnish insurance against sickness and death.

A general business men's club, having a house fronting on Franklin Square, has lately been established, which is recruiting its membership from the superior shop-keepers and clerks of the neighboring streets. This club is interesting as representing a certain degree of local loyalty and common feeling among the middle-class inhabitants of the South End.

There are no independent workingmen's clubs or benefit societies, like those which flourish in England. The labor movement has thrown all its impulse for organization into trade unionism. So largely is this true that it seems extremely difficult for radical or revolutionary groups to hold together. Anarchism is almost unknown. Organized socialist propaganda has never been strong; at present the advocates of Socialism are scattered into several small camps, each bitterly hostile to the others. There is, however, a large amount of undefined socialistic feeling among the rank and file of the trade unions.

The great improvement in all the conditions of labor that has been wrought during recent years is without any possible question the result of working-class organization. The standard wages and the regulation hours of labor in the different trades, to the entire extent that they represent progress for the working classes, have been secured by organized action on the part of the men in those occupations. It may further be stated that, though the trade unions have many faults to answer for, they have on the whole and in the long run distinctly served in bringing about that considerable measure of industrial peace and stability which exists in Boston.

Three fourths of all the trade unions in the city, or about one hundred altogether, meet in this district. These include unions of the skilled and of the unskilled. Unions of the unskilled are few in number, but their membership is very large. The three federal bodies have their headquarters here, — the Central Labor Union, the Building Trades Council, and the Allied Printing Trades Council. The Central Labor Union represents, with a few unimportant exceptions, all organized labor in the city. It adjudicates difficulties that arise between different trade unions, supports them in their complaints against employers when they seem to have good cause, secures City and State action in the interest of working men and women, and assumes a general responsibility for the interests of the wage-earning classes. It now has very solid support and authority; it is still somewhat harassed by the more extreme Socialists in its membership, but the opposition it has met in years past from the Knights of Labor has ceased with the almost complete disappearance of that body in Boston.

Trade unions for women, which are perhaps even more essential than those for men, considering the special moral problems involved, have made only a slight beginning. There is, however, a Union for Industrial Progress, with a large membership, under the direction of an able and devoted working woman, the object of which is to assist working women in the problems that surround their labor, and to train them in methods of trade organization and mutual aid. Several women of leisure give constant sympathy and support to this enterprise. A trade union of laundry workers has been formed under its initiative.

Among the mass of the people actually residing in the district, trade unionism, with the knowledge of industrial conditions and the healthy working-class discontent that go with it, does not have a particularly firm footing. Most of the lodging-house people are a little above its reach; many of the tenement-house people a little below. The unions meet in this locality because it is the most accessible from all parts of the city, not because it is, above other districts, the special stronghold of their membership. Each year nevertheless marks a growth of trade-union sympathy among the people. When there is a street-car strike, local inhabitants cheerfully walk any distance. Employers who are branded by trade unions as unfair gradually become unfair in the eyes of many outsiders too. Membership in a union is much more a thing taken for granted than it used to be even a few years ago. Trade-union labels, which serve to identify to the consumer the products of organized labor, are constantly more in evidence, especially those of the cigar-makers, the printers, the hatters, and the shoe-workers. Several union barber shops exhibit the barber's label in their windows. A number of establishments — too many of them saloons — exhibit the Building Trades Council's certificate, showing that their repairs are done by union workmen. The increasing consideration given by politicians to the labor vote is significant. No political poster or circular appears nowadays without having upon it the trade-union label.

State factory legislation, and the position taken by the City of being a model employer of labor, are both results of the power of the trade unions along with the gradual trend of popular sympathy toward them. This sentiment, in which the present Mayor of Boston, Josiah Quincy, genuinely shares, has led, among other things, to the establishment of municipal departments of electrical construction and general repairs, through which the City does some of its work without contractors. The shops of these departments are in the local manufacturing section. This district also has the most striking and beautiful embodiment of the Mayor's progressive policy, in the Dover Street

Bath House. This is an all-the-year-round bath, with separate departments for men and women. It has accommodated 1400 people in one day. The use of the baths is free, but soap and a towel are furnished for two cents. The building is designed to express something of the dignity of the City, and is the finest public bath house as yet in this country. It stands in interesting contrast with one of the old City swimming baths, a wooden structure, moored each summer to the Dover Street Bridge.

The municipal government is even catching the spirit of that soundly established form of philanthropy which provides wholesome recreation for the people. During the summer of the present year six of the school yards of the district have been kept open for use as playgrounds under competent direction and with suitable appointments. At the same time, under a legacy left in trust to the City, children were taken down the harbor for a day's outing, some of the older boys remaining for a week in camp on one of the harbor islands.

The trustees of that noble municipal institution, the Public Library, on account of the erection of the monumental central building, have been unable as yet to establish a suitable local library in this district. In the meantime there is a little delivery station and reading room on one of the crowded thoroughfares. The residents of one part of the district make some use of the present South End branch library, but it is admittedly in the wrong location, and is poorly adapted to the service which the library administration would gladly render.

All this collective action is bringing about a transformation throughout the entire scheme of social improvement. It suggests that charity and philanthropy must gradually assume a wider form of organization. When the administration of charity, public and private, is largely in the hands of those who have experience of the struggle with poverty; when philanthropy in the full sense works with its constituency instead of for them; when undertakings proved beyond doubt to be for the general good shall be either privately endowed, promoted by popular association, or assumed by the public, — the local district, so far as local influences can determine, will have passed the stage of social recovery and entered upon its normal corporate growth.

# CHAPTER XII

## THE TOTAL DRIFT

A COMMUNITY of forty thousand souls is thus surrounded but not absorbed by a great city. Its life stands for toilsome monotony, rarely reaching distinction save in its tragedies. Yet there is much contentment, often too much. Existence has its joys, and on occasion its gayeties. The young are happy and hopeful. The free spirit, however, is soon bound by the effects of unwholesome surroundings in childhood, joined with the cramping necessities of adult life. A few of the strong willed, together with some brilliant ones that meet with favoring fortune, contrive to triumph over obstacles. All too often these enterprising natures find themselves restricted to the choice between opportunity and rectitude. Weak and inactive natures, if they survive, are likely to relapse into some sort of degradation. The mass of the people is undoubtedly ascending, inch by inch, in the economic and moral scale.

The problem of the district, to a considerable

extent, has to do with racial types adapting themselves to a new and strange environment; but there is among them no inheritance of generations of demoralized ancestry. Native ability is by no means uncommon. There is good reason to believe also that in the essentials of conduct the working people of this locality are on somewhat the same level as people in general. The tenement houses have many instances of devoted family affection. It is impressive and reassuring to find that under much of the home life of the district there is an impregnable rock of fundamental morality. The virtue of generosity and certain aspects of moral courage exist in a high degree. The delicate graces of character and the refinement that goes with elevated companionship are of course lacking.

The average person in such a situation certainly stands in constant need of quickening and uplifting influence; but the important issue does not lie there. A thousand schoolmasters and confessors, a thousand gentle ministrants, — all of the old order, — might alter many scattering lives, while the common life became steadily worse. The individual does not have in himself the main cause of difficulty. In the great majority of cases the trend of his physical and moral existence is practically determined for him by his outward conditions. The real trouble is that people here are from birth at the mercy of great social forces which move almost like the march of destiny.

The chapters which precede undertake to explain the effects which these forces have in the local community upon individual and social life, and to show the various ways in which the restorative energy of the city goes out to meet them. In its official capacity it sets up standards of health, intelligence, and morality, below which the general level of the population cannot fall. It refuses to allow the sick or the hungry to go uncared for. It insists that children shall not grow up in illiteracy. It especially guards some of the chief avenues of degradation. Resting back upon this rudimentary protective system, the people of the city proceed first to see that no family shall be without assistance toward recovering honorably from material disaster, and secondly to supply in general some of the means of a happier and nobler existence. By this voluntary effort additional checks are put on the encroachment of social tendencies upon personal and domestic welfare.

Moreover, some of the larger local affairs are being positively ordered and directed toward beneficent ends. Ward politics and popular amusements, it is true, still run at will, but there are solid developments of helpful association in the sphere of industry. The municipality, too, is passing from merely guarding against evil into urging on the common good. Education and religion not only strengthen individual character from within against harmful conditions, but endeavor directly to counteract the effects of disturbed domestic, industrial, and racial relations.

All of these interests as they affect the district, whether of distinct or of dubious value, have an energy by no means spent. It is safe to expect considerable results in the immediate future along the line of present tendencies, — especially if one takes into account the existing results of the immediate past. As to some of these future results it may reasonably be asked, What ought they to be? There are other larger developments as to which the present inquiry must be content simply to ask, Whither?

The first step with a difficult equation is the elimination of certain factors. No civilized community undertakes to carry within its corporate life the criminal and the lunatic. The South End attempts to carry three equally dangerous types, — the confirmed pauper, the confirmed prostitute, the confirmed drunkard. It can only be a laggard social sense that would have it so. Persons of

these types, who now go to and from the harbor
institutions an incredible number of times, must
be dealt with upon the principle of the habitual
criminal act, the length of term rapidly increasing
with each commitment, and reaching ere long a
sentence that will last until the persons either are
cured or die.   Along with this, there ought to be
— and experience in Boston supports the plan —
an offer given to the winds, to the effect that
every wanderer may, and must, get his meals and
lodging in Boston by hard work.   This would put
the city on every tramp's black list, and would
relieve the South End of the cheap lodging-house
incubus.   A third and equally obvious step in this
connection would be the destruction of at least a
dozen dark, noisome, rear-tenement buildings, such
as open into narrow passageways and blind alleys.
This action would dispose of the most fertile
breeding places of pauperism and its accompanying degradation.   It is encouraging to know that
the Board of Health, under new and sufficient
powers, is moving in this direction.

So much of the social wreckage must be dredged
out.   Any other course with this class itself is
hopeless; and it is blundering to confront the main
issue without having thus cleared the way.   Whatever may be said about the other problems of the

district, that of the treatment of its most degraded types is by no means an insoluble one. Half the reach of mind, application and resource that go into any of the city's great commercial enterprises would in reasonable time effectually settle it.

With these types and their contagion gone, the work of organizing charity would be freed of its most anxious constraints, and could meet exhaustively the needs of the deserving poor, the victims of sickness or misfortune. The honest unemployed, no longer confused with the loafer or the vagabond, could be given work or, failing that, provisional assistance by the City, without his being involved in the disgrace that now goes with overseer's aid. Only the industrious would remain to grow old; and the aged, when under necessity, could, with little fear of demoralizing the younger generation, be pensioned under a veteran's discharge. With the worst fathers and mothers removed, and those with like tendencies threatened by a similar fate, the work of child saving would be greatly simplified. It would not be too much to expect that, with our varied and effective child-saving organizations, the situation would be so girt about that no child exposed to special danger could escape receiving appropriate care.

It is impossible to suggest the sense of relief

which would penetrate all the tenement - house neighborhoods if the occasional besotted husband and father were by merciful justice taken away. The saloon would, of course, still remain; but once branded by law as the entrance to a bottomless pit, larger numbers of novices would be repelled from its door. Already it is possible to detect among young men connected with clubs at settlements and similar centres a pervading feeling that the saloon is a place beneath their self-respect. This suggests how all forms of social activity in the district are serving as counter-irritants to the saloon — to those who have not become its patrons. It would be a mistake, however, to think there can be any substitute for the saloon so far as those who frequent it are concerned. Only a doctrinaire would ask for no-license in this district; but saloon-hotels ought to be abolished. That they compete with illicit liquor-selling is not a sufficient argument to justify them. Farther than that the mere repressive influence of law cannot go at present. However, a system like that of Norway which, through public action, takes away the incentive of private gain, would surely be a great blessing. Indeed, the Boston saloon, in its freedom from the evils that go with secrecy, with allied enticements, and with a lounging, disorderly crowd, as well as in its occasional tendency to discourage outright drunkenness, represents a step toward the comparatively unobjectionable Norwegian drinking place.

As to prostitution, the removal of the most abandoned types would mean at least so much clear gain to the district and to the individuals themselves most concerned. For the rest, it has been a helpful move to use the full power of the law in scattering the nests of vice, and making it more inaccessible.[1] To be sure, other districts, in which reside the well-to-do, have to some extent been invaded ; but why should prostitution be confined to neighborhoods inhabited by working people? It is certainly as much loathed by tenement-house dwellers as by any class in the community. To a remarkable degree they keep their skirts untouched by it, though it is all around them. Certain aspects of it go with the life of part of the lodging houses. But this evil, in its larger aspect, does not spring out of local conditions. What is seen here is the effect, not the cause. All that can be done, therefore, at this point of attack, is to make the downward path a

[1] A striking confirmation of this view is furnished by the marked falling off in the case trade in wine throughout this part of the city.

little more difficult, the upward more inviting. No profound change can ever come until there is more of ethical idealism and a more heroic type of personal morality among respectable people of all classes. Prostitution does not propagate itself; it would quickly work its own destruction.

The different delinquent elements, happily, constitute a rather small fraction of the local inhabitants. The problem which makes the distinctive challenge of the district to the open mind is not that of moral degeneracy. It has to do only incidentally with the quality in a community that is morbid and pathological. It is not even the problem of poverty. Only one fourth of the people are in the strict sense poor.[1] It is the problem of a virile, heterogeneous, undeveloped working population.

It is with such people that a more thorough-going system of education is most needed and is most pregnant with possibilities. Present opportunities are great in amount and variety, but are deficient in substantial value. The manual-training scheme of the public schools needs to be filled out; and it should be completed with a Domestic Arts High School to correspond to the Mechanic Arts High School. It is very important that there

---

[1] Families having less than $10 a week may be called poor.

should be free scholarships to enable promising children of working people to continue their education beyond the grammar - school stage. The waste of ability among the boys and girls of this district for the lack of such scholarships is matter of distinct public concern.

The total volume of effort toward softening and moralizing human nature, toward fitting men and women for useful occupation and good citizenship, is so great as to affect the larger local life. Churches, schools, and philanthropic centres are gradually beginning to see the influence they have poured into the lives of individuals having an effect on families. Influence with different families soon begins to spread through the neighborhoods in which they live. Workers in different neighborhoods find the widening ripples of their influence coalescing with one another. This remarkable social result is not merely because of the complicated relations that go with the life of the district; it is because, more and more, all kinds of religious, educational and general philanthropic effort are done with a distinctly social purpose. It need hardly be said that this does not mean any the less heart-felt personal consideration than went with the old individualist motive. Only with the man's social bonds in mind can one come to terms with the complete personal life. The settlements in their philanthropic work go farthest with the social method, yet it is they which establish the most natural relations with the individual.

It is well that the different philanthropic centres have had an independent, integral development, but there should now be a somewhat compact federation so as to enable them systematically to cover the ground. Such an alliance has existed in fact though not in name, including the South End House, Denison House, Wells Memorial Institute, and Lincoln House. A regularly constituted organization could take in hand the needs of the district as a whole ; could see that neglected corners are looked after ; could advise against the establishment of new centres which would only reduplicate existing efforts ; could unite in certain imposing undertakings in the name of the district as a whole ; and, seeking the coöperation of local citizens, could serve as voluntary trustees of the higher educational and moral interests of the community.

In this federation, also, the churches should wish to be represented. Those churches which are widening their scope so as more broadly to touch human need deserve much praise ; but all the churches cannot do that. It is not desirable that they should. In a district like this, where religious interchange is made impossible by age-long inherited tradition, there is only one way in which religious devotion can be solidly brought to bear for the common welfare. Let the rule be that each church remain the shrine to which men, according to their different minds, shall come for solace and inspiration. Then let certain select spirits from each church, whom others shall be called upon to follow, make it a test of devotion to join with groups from other churches thereabout with the essentially religious purpose of conspiring together for the greater reign of righteousness in that particular vicinity. The reaction of such a policy upon the church would give a wholesome reality to religion by making it the motive power of present-day usefulness.

Already among religious forces there is harmony to the extent that proselytism is generally avoided, not only in connection with all sorts of social work, but even in definite religious propaganda. In the matter of poor relief, Protestants, Catholics, and Jews work in agreement and sometimes in active coöperation. Philanthropic effort among the tenement-house population, which is of course largely in the hands of persons connected with the Protestant churches of the city, is carried on with constant respect for the convictions of Catholics and Jews; and since this has become clearly understood there is little or no opposition from either source. Some of the younger priests and rabbis are indeed distinctly friendly to such undertakings. There is ground for hope that with animosities and misunderstandings removed, there may develop some more positive combination of churches together with the other moral forces of the district.

Such a federation might see that the full enforcement of law is persevered in; that is, for instance, it could stand by a certain local police captain, an irreproachably honest man, who is mysteriously opposed on account of his "bluntness." It might secure the active interest of sagacious business men in practical economic experiments which should endeavor to improve or displace existing tenement and lodging houses, restaurants and saloons, pawnshops and installment stores, theatres and dance halls, by model establishments conducted upon a self-sustaining basis. It could take up the task which the settlements are striving to accomplish, that of bringing those closer forms of influence that deal with family and neighborhood life into relation with the wider, more masculine interests that go with politics and the organization of labor. It might, in the local interest, come into intelligent relation with the municipal administration, securing the full value of its ordinary service, and supporting the larger policy by which the municipality is adapting itself to the new facts in city life.

To pass from such efforts, suggestive and promising as they are, to the various forms of independent organization that exist in the South End, is to come to what is often crude and blundering, like most human interests a tangle of good and evil, but what represents the common people developing their own native abilities and slowly waking to their overwhelming collective power. The training in democracy given by their clubs, lodges, political gangs, and trade unions is producing a strong if not unerring social sense as affecting their economic and political affairs. To a certain extent the Roman Catholic church, in addition to its very great moralizing influence upon the individual, is a co-ordinating force. Though in its official relations the laity have no voice, yet there is an increasing number of organizations loosely associated with the church which are in the hands of the people themselves.

The great variety of organizations in the district serves to bridge in this way and that the gulfs of

distinction in blood and faith which so hinder the
progress of common feeling and loyalty among
workingmen in this country. Indeed, it is true
here, as it is everywhere, that there is. an ethical
tendency in the very fact of association. Whenever men meet together in a self-respecting way
for any legitimate purpose, they learn afresh, from
their very attempt to work together, that the moral
law is the only practical scheme of human intercourse. Moreover, all the variety of organization
will in due time supply a network in which may
be wrought a distinct "new synthesis" of what is
best in the common life. The politician has already discerned the meaning of this; he deftly
turns nearly every form of organization to his
base ends. In due time there will be disinterested
reformers as clever. But even without the self-
conscious reformer, even in spite of the self-seek-
ing politician, these organizations themselves will
come, by that strange upward pressure of association, into the light of higher motives that they
wot not of. Down in the life of the district itself
hopeful forces are gathering, which in the comparison belittle all the efforts of philanthropists
and reformers.

The labor movement is constantly gaining
strength and momentum. Indeed, it is now at a

stage where there is danger of the intoxication of power, and it may have to go backward in order to learn how to go forward gradually. The trade unions constitute an increasing force in the direction of a municipal programme as distinct from national party politics; and though their proposals are not always wise, yet they are in this capacity an indispensable agency for the political training of their constituency. It must be said distinctly, however, that politics to them means something which concerns itself closely with social welfare. In this, if they depart to some extent from the patriotic traditions of the past, they are without doubt moving toward the greater patriotism of the future. Before this tendency, itself strongly imbued with Socialism, the revolutionary type of Socialism is fast being swept away. In one of the trade unions which is largely made up of immigrants, and has all along been aggressively socialist, the Socialists have recently been completely routed in a controversy called up by the Cuban War. The trade unions are in fact making a contribution toward Americanizing the foreign population which is second in value only to that of the public schools. Educationally this contribution is considerable; economically its value is inestimable. Unless the outer intrenchment of a fair standard of life for the working classes can be held, all that is distinctively American will be lost. The trade union insists that the immigrant must not accept any lower condition ; it thus effectually prevents him from undermining the best of our national economic defenses. The foes, however, are not all from without. The workingman's standard of life is constantly threatened by a confused industrial system. Reduction of wages — representing a meaner home, a more burdened wife, more tempted children — is always imminent. The trade unions give themselves unremittingly to warding off this attack upon the citadel of labor.

Local politics, to sheer civic rectitude, would seem almost beyond hope. There are unmistakable signs, however, that the informal social organizations of the district, touched by the many enlightening influences about them, are learning to use their collective political power for their collective interest rather than for the aggrandizement of the boss. From this point it is not so long a step to some appreciation of the general good of the city ; and the step will be taken as soon as the municipality comes to stand more obviously for the particular good of the great masses of its citizens. It has been clearly shown that the boss system has its power by holding up before people whose lives at best are meagre the alluring chance of tangible benefits. The cheat of this can all be exposed by a municipal policy which, with the regularity and impartiality of public service, undertakes to minister more largely to certain keenly felt common needs. In the meantime, nothing need be expected in this district from any vague cry of " municipal reform ; " for that means merely the political notions and, mistakenly or not, the political self-interest of a distant superior class.

The reserve force of the city begins to assert itself definitely against some of the rank developments associated with phenomenal growth. Gradually the incoherent masses that make up the city population are being bound together by a strong municipal government. Such a city government must undertake many new responsibilities. Fortunately at this juncture Boston has a chief executive who looks to the depths of his problem and has rare administrative genius to devote to it. The increasing tendency of the city government in Boston is to concern itself closely with the great common interests of the people. The schools, the public library with its radiating local centres, the board of health, the water department, the police, are all entering upon aggressive methods, with the social well-being in view ; instead of following the old perfunctory way of simply serving the individual needs that made themselves manifest.

Moreover the present Mayor is putting into crystallized form this principle that the administration of modern cities must more and more be socialized. Besides the repair and electrical construction shops already mentioned, there are a printing office and two laundries, all under municipal control, through which the City does its own work in those lines.

In addition, there is a new and active department of public music, giving concerts summer and winter; the art commission is to provide for the decoration of school rooms, and will share in giving the South End Free Art Exhibition; and series of evening lectures, under municipal direction, are to be given in school halls throughout the city. The bath commission is engaged upon a programme which, taking its beginning with the municipal floating and beach baths that have existed for many years, is about to give each working-class section of the city a bath-house open the year round, a playground, to be flooded for skating in the winter, and a gymnasium, all under municipal auspices.

The South End, for reasons that have already been sufficiently expressed, will profit most especially by this humane and realistic policy. What must further come, however, is a greater degree of local autonomy. South End people are justly proud of what the City is accomplishing in their midst. They are not slow to appreciate such efforts to improve their lot. But more of their own representatives must be taken into the confidence of the administration. They must be intrusted with some active responsibility in connection with the schools, the relief of the poor, and the general public care of the local public welfare. In due time, by making the government of the city a personal interest to many local citizens, it would be possible to develop a spirit of dissatisfaction with the men who are now sent as delegates to the City Council.

The reëstablishment of a degree of local self-government in this great district is positively necessary, not only for the political training of citizens, but for securing the local identity and local loyalty out of which the feeling of social responsibility springs. American democracy does not contemplate the formation of vast, sprawling, formless masses of population governed from a single centre. Great cities, under social as well as political necessity, must restore to their local districts some of the old village powers. In this particular district, a partial embodiment, both social and political, of this policy may soon be made in a building which it is proposed to erect on a large lot of ground close to the most crowded corner in the district and owned by the City. At present there is a disused school house on this lot, which beside other things is the chief centre for political gatherings in the district. Such a building as the one proposed would have in it a voting place, certain City offices, headquarters for the central trade-union bodies, a branch of the public library, and a large hall for lectures, concerts, picture shows, and public meetings.[1]

Within the twenty-five years just passed the movement of population has completely changed the face of the South End. Migration into it and out of it seems to be its fate. The coming years will undoubtedly bring a large accession to the Jewish and Italian colonies in this part of the city as people are driven out of the North End by the inroads of wholesale business. The Jews will ere long be very heavy landholders in the district. The more progressive among the Irish are passing on as far as Dorchester, where they

[1] The Mayor has suggested this as a way of using part of the Franklin Fund, which has accumulated from a bequest of Benjamin Franklin to the town of Boston.

live in small flats having open space about them. Many of the rest will retreat to the nearer strongholds of their nationality in Lower Roxbury.

The elevated railway, soon to be built, will make it still easier for mechanics and artisans to transfer their homes to the suburbs. The lodging houses will become lower in grade, and many of them will be turned into tenement houses. There is likely to be much more manufacturing in this district, but not more trade. It used to be thought that the business of the city was tending gradually toward the South End, but within three or four years it has taken a decisive turn toward the west. The moving of the new railroad terminal a half dozen blocks to the north tends still further to keep large commercial enterprise away. There is no likelihood, however, that the district will become isolated. The traffic through its streets will even be greater, as the elevated railroad will undoubtedly do much to develop all the southern growth of the city. A new thoroughfare will have to be cut through, destroying Pleasant Street, to connect the great docks which will be built in South Boston with the increasing number of factories in Cambridgeport.

At the present time practically all the building space in the district is covered. It is hardly con-

ceivable that there should be any more rear tenements. Many of the better buildings, however,
falling into the hands of poorer people, will have
their rooms more crowded. To counteract this
it will in due time be found necessary to clear
all insanitary areas and ground now completely
covered with wooden stables and sheds, running
streets through or making small open spaces.
The class of people living in residences and apartments will be likely to grow less. The better
grades of lodging - house inhabitants will pass
across the western and southern borders of the
district. The lower order of lodging houses will
be scattered indiscriminately among tenement
houses. The preponderance of unskilled workers
will be still greater. Economically the district
will be poorer ; but morally it will be better off.
Its amusements, and even its dissipations, will
settle to the level of the local life.

These kaleidoscopic shiftings of men and conditions will be, however, only the more outward
signs of a slow but mighty underlying movement.
Such a district is created by it, and marks its fateful outcome. Relentless influences of evil break in
upon the people. Unparalleled energies of good
are striving to heal the breach. Infinitely more
than both, able to carry them away before it, is the

great central current that comes with the common life. One is thrilled with the dangers, the blessings, which it bears; its certain meaning is irresistible change. It does not have its sources in the original characters of the local inhabitants. Its tributaries do not take their rise in the spontaneous institutions and customs of the district. Here the stream may be studied so far as to measure the level it seeks, the momentum with which it is driven. Here it may be directed so far as to erect dikes, open sluiceways, and keep the channel clear. The overmastering forces which urge it on, like the tide and gravity, come from the world outside. They belong with the great city, with modern industry, with civilization.

# INDEX

The Riverside Press
CAMBRIDGE, MASSACHUSETTS, U. S. A.
ELECTROTYPED AND PRINTED BY
H. O. HOUGHTON AND CO.